European History

A Captivating Guide to the History of Europe, Starting from the Neanderthals Through to the Roman Empire and the End of the Cold War

Free Bonus from Captivating History (Available for a Limited time)

Hi History Lovers!

Now you have a chance to join our exclusive history list so you can get your first history ebook for free as well as discounts and a potential to get more history books for free! Simply visit the link below to join.

Captivatinghistory.com/ebook

Also, make sure to follow us on Facebook, Twitter and Youtube by searching for Captivating History.

Contents

INTRODUCTION 1

CHAPTER 1 – PREHISTORY..3

CHAPTER 2 – THE NEOLITHIC REVOLUTION 6

CHAPTER 3 – THE BRONZE AGE 10

CHAPTER 4 – EARLY TRIBES OF EUROPE 15

CHAPTER 5 – THE IRON AGE...19

CHAPTER 6 – PREHISTORIC BRITAIN 24

CHAPTER 7 – THE CLASSICAL GREEKS 28

CHAPTER 8 – THE ROMAN EMPIRE 33

CHAPTER 9 – THE VIKINGS 38

CHAPTER 10 – THE DARK AGES 43

CHAPTER 11 – THE HOLY ROMAN EMPIRE........................48

CHAPTER 12 – THE RISE OF WESSEX 52

CHAPTER 13 – THE NORMAN CONQUEST 56

CHAPTER 14 – MARCO POLO AND RENAISSANCE ITALY...62

CHAPTER 15 – JOAN OF ARC 67

CHAPTER 16 – ISABELLA I OF CASTILE 72

CHAPTER 17 – THE AGE OF DISCOVERY............................77

CHAPTER 18 – THE REFORMATION....................................81

CHAPTER 19 – THE ENLIGHTENMENT 86

CHAPTER 20 – THE FRENCH REVOLUTION 90

CHAPTER 21 – THE INDUSTRIAL AGE 97

CHAPTER 22 – THE BRITISH EMPIRE OF QUEEN VICTORIA 103

CHAPTER 23 – THE GREAT WAR...107

CHAPTER 24 – THE RUSSIAN REVOLUTION 112

CHAPTER 25 – WORLD WAR II..116

CHAPTER 26 - THE COLD WAR ERA...123

EPILOGUE 129

Introduction

Europe.

A relatively tiny continent but still one of the most vital on the world stage. Since the days of Neanderthal toolmakers and Cro-Magnon culture, Europe has been a unique center for thriving human communities. Boasting a diverse landscape, this corner of the world became home to Mediterranean traders and seafarers, early wheat farmers, ironsmiths, hunters, kings, queens, religious zealots, hillforts, castles, Latin, democracy, literature, and theater all within the space of a mere few thousand years. Human civilization blossomed in all parts of Europe, whether they were the cold, wet stretches of Scandinavia, the rocky cliffs of Greece, or the Russian plains.

The history of people in Europe is a fascinating one that starts, as most do, with hunters, gatherers, and fishermen that eventually explode into a kaleidoscope of niche cultures—each with its own gods, goddesses, food staples, and building techniques. Initially quite isolated from one another, the people of Europe evolved intricate social systems and relationships with one another that eventually bonded them through trade and marriage. They built farms, villages, cities, and entire empires to protect their cultures and convert others to their ways of thinking, only to have it all crumble under the strength of the next warlord.

Europe's past is characterized by fighting and warfare, and it is punctuated with great works of art, philosophy, science, and technology. Even its recent history is much the same—that's why so much of the globe was once ruled by European monarchies. Despite all the infighting and territorial exploits, Europeans have managed to create some of the most beautiful pieces of literature, architecture, political structures, and ideas the world has ever seen.

Chapter 1 – Prehistory

Despite their heavy skeletons and developed brow ridges, Neanderthals were probably little different from modern humans. Some of the skeletal remains appear to be from deliberate burials, the first evidence for such careful behaviour among humans.

(*Encyclopedia Britannica*)

Prehistory is the period of time before any written history. We have some idea of what happened then from the remains that have been and continue to be studied and analyzed.

As the story of human history always does, Europe's story begins with hominids—those bipedal descendants of the great apes who learned how to craft simplistic tools, clothe themselves in the skins of dead animals, and even cook their scavenged meals over the hot flames of a controlled fire. These human ancestors wandered into Europe from Africa via the Middle East about 45,000 years ago.[1] Back then, there were multiple species and cultures of humanity, including the Neanderthal and Cro-Magnon, both of whom made their homes throughout Europe. Neanderthals far predated the Cro-Magnons, however; they'd actually evolved in Europe about 350,000 years before ever setting eyes on their Cro-Magnon cousins.

Within just a few thousand years of modern humans' appearance in

---

[1] Ninan, M. M. *The Development of Hinduism*. 2008.

Europe, the Neanderthal branch of the human family completely disappeared. No one knows exactly why this happened, but there are two popular theories. The first posits that Homo sapiens clashed violently with their Neanderthal neighbors, killing and wiping out the offending populations of the latter group. The second theory suggests that Neanderthals and Cro-Magnons simply interbred to the point that they became one civilization and culture instead of two. There is evidence for this in the existence of Neanderthal DNA mixed into the DNA of Cro-Magnon humans as well as even modern humans.

Whatever the early social order of Europe's first people, the Cro-Magnon emerged as the only remaining species and laid its claim boldly to the continent during a period when the climate was particularly cold. Research from some archaeologists has suggested that the social structure of the Cro-Magnon was particularly advantageous to humans at that time since they could gain access to resources over a larger area thanks to community sharing and trade.

The lone human survivors of that nasty cold snap about 40,000 years ago wrapped themselves liberally in furs and skins and pressed onward. They learned to live in small communities, traveling from place to place as hunter-gatherers.[2] Nomadic by nature, it was the daily ambition of these people to search for deer, fish, root vegetables, seeds, acorns, sea beets, and honey. Though their primary goal was big game or seafood, hunter-gatherers of Mesolithic Europe were not picky. They ate vegetable matter whenever and wherever they could find it, a habit that not only provided them with necessary vitamins and fiber but with the instruments of reasonably healthy teeth.[3] Grass seeds, the predecessors to cereals like wheat, oats, and barley, were frequently included in meals.

---

[2] Peregrine, P.N. and Ember, M. – Editors. *Encyclopedia of Prehistory.* 2001

[3] Hansen, V. and Curtis, K. *Voyages in World History – Third Edition.* 2016.

Despite their strong teeth and bones, however, Cro-Magnons only lived into their 30s or 40s, if they even survived infancy. Over the course of the next 30,000 years, their numbers increased minimally as it was difficult to manage large families in a nomadic system. All of that was about to change, however, as the next step in human evolution was just around the corner.

Chapter 2 – The Neolithic Revolution

The word agriculture, after all, does not mean "agriscience," much less "agribusiness." It means "cultivation of land." And cultivation is at the root of the sense both of culture and of cult. The ideas of tillage and worship are thus joined in culture. And these words all come from an Indo-European root meaning both "to revolve" and "to dwell." To live, to survive on the earth, to care for the soil, and to worship, all are bound at the root to the idea of a cycle.

(Wendell Berry, *The Art of the Commonplace*)

The Neolithic Revolution can also be called the Agricultural Revolution as it was the transitioning of the hunter-gatherers into a more settled lifestyle which was based on agriculture.

Stone Age hunter-gatherers across Europe had known for centuries how seeds worked, but they'd never had any motivation to sit down and start planting gardens. It is difficult to determine what convinced prehistoric Europeans to settle down, build permanent homes, and start farming, but DNA and archaeological research suggest it was the product of cultural mixing.

The first evidence of farming in Europe comes from Greece and Turkey, and it can still be found in the form of agricultural terracing. Terracing is a method of agriculture that is often employed in rocky, hilly landscapes. In place of flat, vast fields, the early peoples of this southeastern corner of Europe created a series of steps on mountainsides and hills, separated and fortified by short stone walls. It was about 8,500 years ago that families began planting grains and vegetables this way in the Mediterranean.[4]

These are the earliest forms of agriculture archaeologists have found in Europe, but even more information on the cultural change from gathering to farming has been discovered hidden away in the DNA of modern Europeans. Genetic markers show that at that point in prehistory, new DNA was introduced to Europe's population simultaneously with cereal crops. It is clear that peoples whose culture already included farming methodology migrated into Turkey and Greece 8,500 years ago, settling there and starting families with the local people.

As far as archaeological evidence can tell us, the original Neolithic period began in the Middle East, in the piece of land where the Euphrates and Tigris Rivers meet in what is now Iraq but what was once ancient Mesopotamia. Both rivers begin within 50 kilometers (31 miles) of one another in Turkey, meaning that the Agricultural Revolution could have literally followed the span of these rivers in Turkey, where it traveled a short distance over land and sea to take hold in Greece. From there, it spread northwestward across the rest of Europe.

The movement of the Neolithic Revolution was determined but slow. Traditional hunter-gatherers were not convinced they should settle in one place and completely change their lifestyle, despite the popularity of agriculture along the Mediterranean. The entire continent of Europe is comprised of 9,938,000 square kilometers (3,837,081 square miles) and vast differences in climate.[5] the mild weather of the Mediterranean may have been conducive to farming for the Greeks and Turks, but the methods imported from Mesopotamia wouldn't

---

[4] Brennan, S and Withgott, J. *Environment: The Science Behind the Stories.* 2005.

[5] "Europe." *World Atlas.* Web.

have been successful in the dry cold of northern climes.

Farming was still very much a new technology, and it took several thousand years for it to be adapted to different regions. One of the most important developments to flourish alongside farming was that of animal husbandry, whereby people learned to domesticate and keep small herds of animals instead of hunting. Goat, sheep, pigs, and cows proved the easiest to domesticate, and thus, these became the meat staples for most European farmers. With the ability to keep livestock within reach, suddenly the benefits of a sedentary lifestyle became clear to western and northern families and small communities.

Wheat, barley, lentils, peas, and beans proved to be the most reliable crops, accounting for their use from Greece to the British Isles about 5,000 years ago.[6] as these seeds were dispersed across the continent, so too were domesticated animals. As humans became more knowledgeable concerning their livestock, they began to use them for milk as well as meat. The first evidence for cheese-making—an arguable cornerstone of modern European culture—comes from about 7,000 years ago in Poland.[7] at a Neolithic site in Kujawy, archaeologists have found clay pottery bowls made with holes, as if to strain curds from whey. The pottery was tested in a lab and came up positive for milk fats.

Farms and animal husbandry were delicate economic systems that relied fundamentally on the fertility of each region and landscape. The diffusion of such technology across Europe was initially dependent on mild weather and mineral-rich, river-adjacent land that could support their selected plant varieties. While humankind experimented with farming techniques, the plant strains evolved rapidly due to human selection and changing growing conditions. The einkorn and millet of Mesopotamia changed into bulkier cereal grains with a stronger rachis, which is the part of the plant that connects the seed to the stalk.

Given all the potential complications, farming was not a viable option for many families in Neolithic Europe. For several thousand years, hunter-gatherers, farmers, and pastoralists (sheep or cattle owners) lived as neighbors throughout the continent, interacting and even

---

[6] Sage Reference. *"The SAGE Encyclopedia of Economics and Society."* Web

[7] Donnelly, C. Editor. *The Oxford Companion to Cheese.* 2016

intermarrying. As farming techniques became more precise and localized, home settlements became more characteristic of the realm and more appealing to people whose livelihoods required them to walk great distances for food. As the homesteads of farming people began to dot the landscape more heavily, they eventually overcame the resistant hunter-gatherer culture altogether.

What followed was an unprecedented population boom followed by a population crash.[8] the excess food made available by intensive growing methods made it possible for families to grow larger than ever before. Scientific testing of Neolithic populations in Europe shows that fertility rates of farming families also became higher. Both these factors explain the increase in the population during the Neolithic age, but they may also shed some light on the later crash as well. Once Europe's carrying capacity was breached—that is, the land's potential food output was outweighed by human numbers—it would appear scarcity and disease took hold of those prehistoric peoples until a balance could be achieved again.

By about 3000 BCE, European peoples were fairly settled. Decidedly a farming culture at that point, they started to build villages, public buildings, and religious temples that would last for millennia.[9] in scattered populations of prehistoric Europeans regathering their strength, the first vestiges of what we might recognize as European culture appeared for the first time.

[8] Bodley, J.H. *Anthropology and Contemporary Human Problems – Fifth Edition.* 2008

[9] Milisauskas, S. Editor. *European Pre-history – A Survey – 2nd Edition.* 2011

Chapter 3 – The Bronze Age

Suddenly and decisively the impressive megalithic tombs of western Europe are set earlier than any comparable monuments anywhere approaching them in antiquity.

(Colin Renfrew, *Before Civilization*)

With the Neolithic Revolution firmly under way, the Bronze Age began. This was when humans learned to melt copper and tin together into bronze, a brand-new, super-strong metal. Bronze could fill a multitude of roles that were previously filled by tin, bones, wood, or rocks. It was a game changer for the communities of early Europe, and it had the potential to revolutionize farming, food preparation, weaponry, and warfare.

The new technology spread easily. The Mediterranean Sea was a source of much cultural inspiration thanks to its proximity to North Africa, Europe, and West Asia. Seafaring peoples from Egypt, Morocco, Turkey, Greece, and Italy built canoes and then galley ships, which were capable of making long-distance voyages across the sea. They met one another at their urban capitals and port towns of Piraeus, Heracleion, and Paphos to trade copper, tin, grains, vegetables, fish, pottery, and stone receptacles. The Greeks already had copper, but they needed supplies of tin to create the new alloy, and therefore, their relationship with other members of the Mediterranean was more important than ever.

Unlike the western and northern farming villages of Europe, with each only home to 100 people at most, many towns of early Greece had as many as 2,000 people.[10,11] These were fortified towns, surrounded by strong stone walls to keep out potential enemies from within and outside Greece.[12] Even as bronze tools and decorative pieces overtook the ancient land of Hellas (the early name for Greece), stone remained incredibly important to its civilization. Stone walls held back violent conquering tribes and provided homes for families, and stone was also still used for tool-making.

Ancient Grecians of the Bronze Age had lived in large communities long enough to know that outsiders posed a constant threat to their safety and valuable goods. With that mindset, metalworkers cast strong spears, knives, solid shields, helmets, and chest plates to protect soldiers tasked with keeping their cities safe. The weaponry and defensive items also came in handy when city leaders found themselves in land disputes with nearby chieftains and landowners.

On the island of Crete nearby, the Minoan people were responsible for most of the seafaring technology and trading routes of that corner of Europe and West Asia. They flourished during the Bronze Age thanks to their crucial position at the marine crossroads of so many different peoples. At their cultural height, the Minoans built palaces four stories in height, installed complex plumbing systems, and created their own written language. They may well have led the world into the Classical Antiquity Age if it hadn't been for the eruption of Santorini in about 1500 BCE.[13] The damage, death, and devastation following the eruption proved impossible to overcome, and the Minoans

---

[10] *Audouze, Francoise and* Olivier Büchsenschütz. *Town, Villages and Countryside of Celtic Europe.* 1992.

[11] Bintliff, J. *The Complete Archeology of Greece.* 2012.

[12] Bintliff, J. *The Complete Archeology of Greece.* 2012.

[13] University of Rhode Island. *"Santorini eruption much larger than originally believed."* 2006.

disappeared from the archaeological record. Their DNA, however, is still present in the genetic data obtained from modern Greeks.[14]

At this time, Britain, France, and Germany got to work forging bronze farming tools with which to plow and sow the soil more effectively. The invention of the plow had a significant and very positive impact on European agriculture, and it was thanks to the new, strong, and durable metal that those ancient, simplistic devices did the job required of them. Now, with heavy axes and sharp blades, clearing the land of its woods and forests became less exhausting and burdensome. Not only could fields be cleared quicker, but they could now be maintained better. Breaking into the topsoil and aerating it—a process necessary to prepare the soil for seeds—was much less laborious with a bronze plow at the ready. With these advancements, crop yields increased.

Agriculture began to completely reshape the face of the land. Woods were felled and replaced with distinct strips of seasonal crops. In regions where the soil was covered by a layer of shale or chalk, these rock formations were painstakingly scraped from the ground and pushed into heavy, long mounds that served as property borders. Their urban centers remained relatively small compared to those of Greece, but cities did indeed begin to dot the landscape and swell into the countryside.

In Britain, the Bell Beaker culture appeared in about 2500 BCE among an influx of Western European migration.[15] The Beaker culture, for short, is an archeological name for the people who used the beaker-style pottery. These beakers were widest at the top, the opposite of jug-style pots which have full bellies and small openings at the top. These types of pottery were often found in graves, which is where

---

[14] Sciscape *"Modern Greeks are the decedents of ancient Mycenaeans"* 2018. Web.

[15] Cummings, V. *The Neolithic of Britain and Ireland.* 2017.

much of the archeological information of the era has been gathered from.

During this age, communities of people now buried their dead loved ones in the earth individually, often placing small items alongside the body. These items included flint blades, pots of porridge, and the defining beaker style pottery. The individuals' graves were marked by earthen mounds, wooden structures, or boulders. The latter came to define the people of Bronze Age Britain and Western Europe in the minds of historians as much as the beakers they used defined them for archaeologists.

Giant stone structures appeared during this time in Britain. The stones were quarried from a variety of locations, including modern Wales and the Marlborough Downs, which probably provided the giant stones needed to create what might be the most famous megalith of all, Stonehenge.[16] The details behind the construction of Stonehenge have been lost to the ages, but the structure still stands to commemorate the civilization which built it—and it's not the only building that harkens back to the Bronze Age. Not far away, in the village of Avebury, dozens of massive boulders mark the ancient path into the community, encircling a prehistoric community center studded by even more stones. At the farthest circle, a hill creates the outer border for the town.

Stone and wooden henges were built in Ireland, Britain, France, Wales, and Scotland by a widespread culture which probably used them as religious temples and possibly even astronomical calendars. Though the people who built these amazing structures don't seem to have had a writing system to use for the historical record, they've left enough of themselves behind to denote a sense of community, family, hierarchy, and growing spirituality. At its height, the Beaker culture stretched all the way from Portugal to Poland, and DNA research

[16] Streiffert, A. – Editor. *The World's Must-See Places*. 2005.

shows that they almost completely overwhelmed the previous cultures of the British Isles.

While megaliths, stylized pottery, and massive tombs characterized the European Bronze Age, population increases and widespread diversification would epitomize the next phase of the continent's cultural evolution. Language, political organization, and urbanization were about to become very important.

Chapter 4 – Early Tribes of Europe

To reach the farthest chamber of Lascaux, it's likely a man had to snuff out his light, lower himself down a shaft with a rope made of twisted fibers, and then rekindle his lamp in the dark so as to draw the woolly rhinoceros, the half horse, and the raging bison there.

(Jane Brox, *Brilliant: The Evolution of Artificial Light*)

The more people that inhabited Europe, the more social strategies came into play. It was necessary for the various communities of farmers, traders, fishermen, craftspeople, and emerging tribal kings to understand one another, which is why at this point the proto-Celtic language was used in the north and eastern parts of Europe. Hellenic languages (pre-Greek) ruled in the south, while the Beaker language—whatever that may have been—dominated the west. Though it is almost certain that dozens of localized, niche languages existed alongside these, it was the communal languages that spread across large regions of the continent.

Determining which cultures were the most influential at the time is a simple matter of following the linguistic patterns. Along the Mediterranean, the language known to researchers as Linear B replaced the lost language of Crete, Linear A.[17] This language slightly preceded ancient Greek and has been deciphered as its immediate ancestor. Clay tablets using the language have been recovered

---

[17] Pullar, A. *Dust of Gods* 2018.

throughout southern Greece and nearby Mediterranean islands.

As for the Beaker people, the lack of written records means their part in the language tree of Europe can't be pinned down with certainty. Linguistic and archaeological research connecting various Beaker communities, however, have been interpreted by many experts to suggest that those ancients spoke a form of Indo-European, possibly the predecessor to the German language.

These findings paint a picture of Bronze Age and Early Iron Age Europe as dominated by proto-Celts, Greeks, and the Beaker people. These three cultures probably had some basic knowledge and skill with the languages of the others, which was necessary for land disputes, cross-tribal marriages and contracts, and, of course, trading.[18] Hellas' people focused mainly on socialization with other members of the Mediterranean Sea, sharing goods, family ties, and political connections with people in Egypt and Turkey. Theirs was a life remarkably different from their western and northern counterparts in Europe, and this was probably due to Greece's relative proximity to Mesopotamia.

Mesopotamia is credited with the creation of humankind's very first cities, writing systems, farms, and large-scale political structures. Though the so-called Cradle of Civilization was nearly 3,000 kilometers (1,865 miles) from Greece, early Thracians from the north of Hellas had been spreading out eastward for centuries, considerably shortening the distance between the two groups of people.

Thracians and Greeks could speak their own languages in the city of Byzantium (now Istanbul in Turkey), around 3,000 years ago.[19] Thus, traders and explorers from Mesopotamia became more interested in visiting the Greco-Thracian city and probably made regular visits,

---

[18] Anthony, D. *The Horse, the Wheel, and Language.* 2007.

[19] Ricks, D. and Magdalino, P. *Byzantium and the Greek Identity.* 2018.

bringing along grain, oil, cloth, and the ideas of a brand-new way of life.

Of course, meetings between the various cultures of Bronze Age Europe were by no means always peaceful. The very definition of that period came about thanks to a great variety of bronze weaponry found in archaeological sites throughout the continent. One such site at the battlefield of Tollense Valley in Germany revealed many secrets about the state of warfare some 3,250 years ago.[20] 130 bodies of men between the ages of 20 and 40 were unearthed there, showing fatal wounds from arrows, spears, and swords. Estimates put the number of fighting men at about 2,000, plus a number of horses.[21]

The domestication of the horse occurred around 3000 BCE, and it became a tool for long-distance travel as well as large-scale warfare.[22] Laboratory analysis of the bones and teeth of the horses and slain warriors from the Tollense Valley site reveal that there were two distinct groups of people involved in the battle: Locals and a group from as far away as the Czech Republic. The newcomers may have been hired mercenary fighters imported by another local chieftain intent on taking control of what looks to have been a populated area. Mercenary warfare was common during this and later eras.

Land disputes were probably the major source of violence between locals and distant communities since a rising population led to more frequent encounters between settled peoples. More diversification between cultures also began to appear at the close of the Bronze Age. This has been determined archeologically in the different ways the

---

[20] Horn, C. and Kristiansen, K. – Editors. *Warfare in Bronze Age Society.* 2018.

[21] Price, T. Douglas et al. "Multi-isotope proveniencing of human remains from a Bronze Age battlefield in the Tollense Valley in northeast Germany." *Springer-Verlag GmbH Germany.* 2017.

[22] Milisauskas, S. Editor. *European Prehistory – A Survey.* 2002.

societies handled their dead.

For example, one group of people ritualistically burned the bodies of their dead and buried them in urns. Known as the Urnfield people, they used specialized tools such as socket axes and palstave axes made of lead.[23] The Urnfield people would soon form into the Hallstatt culture, characterized by cemeteries and a presumed high standard of living for that time period.

The Late Bronze Age also saw the transformation of Wessex in modern England. The people embraced pastoralism wholeheartedly, felling much of the natural woodland to accommodate their herds of sheep, pigs, and cattle. Abundant tin resources in the southern part of the island were in high demand throughout Europe, which meant a regular source of income, trade, and settlers for the ancient Britons. Wealth collected from the mines went to local chieftains and merchants alike, both of whom used it to further develop urban centers. The towns of Western Europe remained relatively tiny in comparison with those of Greece and Western Turkey, but warfare was becoming a way of life for Europeans in all regions of the continent. It would define much of the realm's short-term and long-term future.

---

[23] Boughton, Dot. "The Early Iron Age socketed axes in Britain." July 2015. Retrieved from Academia.edu.

Chapter 5 – The Iron Age

Holding us between repulsion and respect, terror and deference, we're still, it would seem, affected by these gutted husks. Much like the mask of the gorgon, the skulls belong neither to this world nor the next, but to that wavering interface, that intermediary realm between being and non-being, the living and the dead. Threshold figures, they command passage.

(Gustaf Sobin, *Luminous Debris*)

It was about 1200 BCE when another life-changing technology swept Europe, starting at the eastern edge of the continent.[24] It was there that experienced and adventurous metalworkers figured out how to make a new material even stronger than bronze. Using iron ore collected by miners, these craftspeople discovered that by burning the ore at extremely high temperatures, they could remove the impurities in the mineral and purify liquid iron. It was the dawn of the Iron Age.

Iron formation was by no means as simple as crafting alloys of copper and tin. It required groups of metallurgists to build a thick clay oven and keep it stocked with charcoal over the course of several hours. If built and fueled properly, the fire inside those ovens could reach 1300 degrees Celsius (2372 Fahrenheit), a hot enough temperature to crack

---

[24] Milisauskas, S. Editor. *European Prehistory – A Survey.* 2002.

the iron ore and begin to break it down. When the iron ore was superheated, impurities were forced from the emerging metal and burned away. What remained behind was both iron and carbon, which began to pour out of a tap at the bottom of the oven. After several rounds of processing, eventually the carbon and other impurities were burned and hammered away, leaving behind large balls of red-hot iron. The waste material, called slag, was left behind in molten, ashy heaps.

Iron by itself was a rather hit-and-miss effort for prehistoric people experimenting with metallurgy. The best results were often not terribly tougher than bronze, and it was certainly more difficult to process. The advantage to ancient people was that iron ore was widely available throughout Europe, and it did not need to be mixed with another type of metal to create a workable material. There can be little doubt that the craftspeople of the Early Iron Age were confused about the irregular product that flowed from their iron smelting ovens. Dependent on the amount of carbon remaining within the smelted iron, the resulting metal could either be brittle or incredibly strong. Unfortunately, there were little those metallurgists could do to identify the superior pieces of ore.

The Hallstatt people, who were predominately agricultural, were some of the first to embrace the new iron technology, even though it was far from perfect. At first, they almost exclusively used iron for sword making while maintaining their bronze capabilities for daggers and other types of swords.[25] Ironically, for most of the Iron Age, bronze remained the most important metal available to Europeans, who used the material for weapons and a variety of farming tools. Silver and gold were mined alongside tin, copper, and iron ore, but given their extreme flexibility and relative weakness, these were only used decoratively. Of course, the very existence of decorative statues,

---

[25] Clark, G. *World Prehistory – A New Outline.* 1969.

embellished tools and weaponry, and jewelry denotes the emergence of the wealthy class. It can also show the existence of an emerging hierarchy, whereupon the authority of the ruling chieftains rested.

Elite members of the Hallstatt culture tended to live in what is now eastern France and southern Germany. There are two kinds of elite burial sites located in this region: those of warriors and those of political leaders. The former was buried in full bronze armor and the latter with heavy chariots. North of the Alps, powerful local leaders fought their way to the top of the political system, thanks to the employment of hired mercenary armies from other parts of the continent. These leaders built the port city of Marseille from which their seafarers and merchants could more easily reach Greek ports, such as Piraeus.

By trading directly with Greece, the Hallstatt people were able to create a great deal of wealth when they resold goods to the people of the west. Greek goods were very popular for two main reasons: the Greeks were more advanced than the rest of Europe and therefore trendy, and their Mediterranean resources were vastly varied and met both basic and luxury desires. As normal life became peppered with luxury, so too did the graves of the Hallstatt people. Burial chambers, usually built into small, concealed underground chambers and covered over by earthen mounds, contained more and more items over the course of the next millennium.

Cultural traditions were transformed by the influx of immigrants, Mediterranean goods, and the stratification of European civilization. People now had the wealth and worldly perspective to create their own spiritual organizations as a means to explain existence. Spirituality and religion became a central feature of collective culture, with dozens of different interpretations of the universe spreading across the continent. The Hallstatt people and other proto-Celt peoples developed a fixation on skulls and heads of their lost friends and family, as well as those of their slain enemies.[26] It wasn't unheard of for their hunter-gatherer and early farming ancestors to collect skulls, but the fixation became more acute as the Hallstatt people moved into the Late Iron Age; during this period, archaeologists hypothesize that skulls were venerated as personal power tokens. It was at that point they began to distinguish themselves to archaeologists as pre-modern Celts.

Violence as a way of life had a considerable effect on the people of Iron Age Europe, and in no way is this more archaeologically apparent than in the collections of skulls and embalmed heads of the Celts. The "Cult of Skulls," as these various head-collecting people are often called, were powerful enough in terms of warfare and cultural influence that their customs were adopted by Mediterranean Europeans west of Greece and its Ionian islands.[27] It seems as if violence, being the primary means of obtaining land and goods as well as imparting culture upon one's neighbors, came to be both glorified and worshiped.

Perhaps the most lasting image from Europe's Iron Age is the use of an iron sword to separate the head of a Celtic enemy from his body. The heads were anointed with oil or wet clay and placed on altars within public temples, presumably as a display of superiority and power. While the severed heads of Celtic enemies—which likely included many Celts—were often embalmed and put on display so, too, it seems were the heads of lost loved ones. Both types of skulls seem to have had a spiritual and emotional importance to the most dominant people of the Iron Age. Within a thousand years, examples of the Cult of Skulls were found from the British Isles to the Baltic Sea.

---

[26]Nikolova, Lolita; Merlini, Marco, and Alexandra Comsa. *Western-Pontic Culture Ambience and Pattern: In memory of Eugen Comsa.* 2016.
[27] Sobin, G. *Luminous Debris.* 1999.

Though the skull worshipers were directly linked to chariot warfare, they were also founded on a civilization of agriculture. Superior iron smelting techniques didn't just lead to the manufacture of iron swords for war but also heavy, sharp iron plows. Farmers kept their fields aerated and sown to capacity, fully aware that it was their crops and livestock feeding the chieftains, kings, and armies that kept away enemies. While farming families worked hard to provide food for themselves and their protectors, the growing walls of skulls reminded them what was at stake.

Chapter 6 – Prehistoric Britain

The Iron Age was an era of intense development in Wessex, a small realm in the southern-central region of England. About three or four million people are estimated to have lived throughout Britain by the Late Iron Age,[28] around 400 BCE, and most of these were concentrated in the agricultural and cultural center of Wessex. Hill forts, burial chambers, memorial hills, and wooden and stone henges typified the building works of these people, and a great deal of them are still intact today.

To keep an eye on the enemy and protect themselves, kings of early Britain built their homes on hilltops. If the hill was not sufficiently high enough or difficult enough to traverse, they would have a circular ditch dug around the base of it fortified by an earthen wall surrounding that. In the wet seasons, the ditches would be swamped and mucky, making a swift enemy attack impossible. Hillforts dotted the landscape as evidence of the kings' constant paranoia and vigilance.

The Celtic culture and language found a permanent home in the British Isles and came to define that region of Europe despite the fact that dozens of other tribes lived among them. Their language was shared by people inhabiting the small islands surrounding the British mainland and proved ultimately resistant against further cultural assimilation. The Celts depended mostly on their cereal crops of

---

[28] Oosthuizen, S. *Tradition and Transformation in Anglo-Saxon England.* 2013.

wheat, barley, and emmer, which were supplemented with vegetables and, to a smaller extent, milk, cheese, and meat. Their taste in meat was not confined to one or two choices either; chicken, sheep, eggs, pigs, cows, goats, dogs, and fish could be part of the menu. For the most part, however, grains and vegetables filled the bellies of the Celts and their neighboring tribes in the form of bread and stews.

By the 5th and 4th centuries BCE, the Celts and the Hallstatt culture had evolved into the Late Iron Age culture of La Tène, which managed to influence people all across the continent from Ireland to Italy.[29] The archaeological record shows evidence of an entirely new style of artistic craftsmanship that was highly sought after. These decorative items, adorned in gold, silver, and bronze, were exceptionally wrought and often quite delicate. Large, fixed necklaces were particularly popular, and these were crafted from metals that had been embossed with tiny, symmetrical patterns. Golden decorations for shoes were even more fine and delicate, as were the myriad bronze wall-hangings and altar adornments crafted to decorate the spaces around altar alcoves in which skulls were displayed.

Warfare was frequent between the various Britons, but political anxieties calmed somewhat during the Late Iron Age, reducing the number of hillforts. Of those that remained in use, fortifications such as moats, ditches, ringed hills, and stone walls were added. The civilization within the walls was focused on intertribal border policies and quick, defensive military tactics. Outside the walls, farmers and hunters honed their exceptional skills. During that period, Briton farmers were famed as far away as Greece for their immense wheat yields, and their trained hunting dogs. Both were traded near and far, as were Briton slaves.

These slaves were young Britons themselves, sold by their own families after having fallen upon hard times. Slaves were either sold

---

[29] Mountain, H. *The Celtic Encyclopedia – Volume 1.* 1997.

as children to wealthy landowners or were captured during intertribal warfare. Slaves were no rare commodity either; thousands could potentially come under the control of just one nobleman or petty king. As much as ten percent of the total population of Britain was enslaved, though very little documentation or archaeological evidence exists to shed any light on the daily duties of those men, women, and children.[30] Given the economic realities of the day, it seems likely that they were used as farmers as well as in household servitude.

Just like their continental kinsmen, the Iron Age British people had cultivated a lifestyle rich in spiritual and religious meaning.[31] They appear to have attributed feminine and masculine divinity to a variety of objects, including water wells and the sky, which were considered feminine and masculine respectively. Tribes and their communities throughout ancient Britain left behind a wealth of archaeological evidence, not only showcasing their skill at craftsmanship but as a record of the things their Druid priests used to sacrifice to their gods. Many such sacrifices have been recovered in bogs, both in Britain and Western Europe.[32]

A bog, a concentrated wet area too thick to swim in but too watery to stand on, was considered the ideal location for religious ceremonies involving a sacrifice. Dozens of these sites have been used in Britain for a thousand years, and within their depths reside weaponry, slain animals, jewelry, and even human sacrifices. It is possible the people making sacrifices of horses, dogs, people, and various metalworks knew the secret of the bog: that what goes in will remain preserved for millennia. The combination of cold temperatures and lack of

---

[30] *Davis, David Brion. The Problem of Slavery in Western Culture. 1970.*

[31] Ritari, K. and Bergholm, A. – Editors. *Understanding Celtic Religion: Revisiting the Pagan Past.* 2013.

[32] Insoll, T. – Editor. *The Oxford Handbook of the Archaeology of Ritual and Religion.* 2011.

oxygen within the muddy, acidic bog water maintained the animal and artifact sacrifices the Iron Age people of Britain placed into their depths in alarmingly pristine condition. The so-called "bog bodies" of the Late Bronze and Iron Age are, in many cases, still there, mummified with their skin and organs still intact.

The people in the bogs were usually killed with knives or bludgeoning or strangling devices, and some had their heads and bodies separated before being thrown into the mud. Archaeologists posit that the victims of the bog were probably a mixture of slaves—considered expendable by their masters—and criminals found guilty of terrible crimes. These bog people are nearly all that remains of the Druid culture in terms of human bodies since most of the Britons preferred to cremate their dead. Those who did bury their dead in the ground at that time often did so only after removing the flesh, thereby leaving only skeletons and no items to study.

Contemporary scholars, such as the Greeks, wrote that the Druid religion taught Britons the immortality of the soul. Druidism also taught that following death, the soul moved onto a new body to be born again. It was a belief system that mirrored a similar school of philosophy, far away in the burgeoning realm of Greece.

Chapter 7 – The Classical Greeks

Periclean Greeks employed the term idiotis, without any connotation of stupidity or subnormality, to mean simply "a person indifferent to public affairs." Obviously, there is something wanting in the apolitical personality. But we have also come to suspect the idiocy of politicization—of the professional pol and power broker. The two idiocies make a perfect match, with the apathy of the first permitting the depredations of the second.

(Christopher Hitchens, *Prepared for the Worst*)

The ancient lands of Hellas (modern Greece) started to urbanize rapidly between the 8th and 5th centuries BCE.[33] Unlike its Western European counterparts, the early Greeks quickly arranged themselves into large towns to better facilitate commerce and personal safety. Positioned only a week or so away on horseback from Mesopotamia, Greek and other Mediterranean cultures urbanized much more rapidly than those at a great distance from the Middle East.

It was on the western coast of the Hellenistic mainland that the community of Athens was formed upon a high rocky outcrop. The land had been used as pasture and farmland for at least 2,000 years before the town started to grow, and it had been mostly occupied by nomadic families of that area who came together to plant crops of

---

[33] Andersen, Helle Daamgard. *Urbanization in the Mediterranean.* 1997.

barley, wheat, and vegetables.[34] As agriculture proved successful season after season in this part of Greece, more and more of its nomadic farmers decided to make Athens their permanent home.

Athens' appeal had a great deal to do with its location as it was just within reach of the port community of Piraeus. In Piraeus, even more Ionians clustered, encouraged to form permanent settlements due to the regular supplies of fish and seafood they found there. By the 5th century BCE, merchants in Piraeus received merchants from other parts of Hellas and the nearer Mediterranean communities who were eager to trade grain, fabrics, wool, pottery, and other items for the olives, oil, salted fish, and surplus foods they found at the port. It was this first consolidation of foodstuffs that helped both Piraeus, Athens, and other similar coastal villages grow and thrive.

By the end of the 5th century BCE, Athens was fully established as the capital of Hellas and one of the major cities of the Mediterranean Basin.[35] Not only was it a rich and beautiful city, centered upon the incomparable marble temples of the Acropolis, but Athens was a democratic city-state in which the first instance of Western democracy was practiced. Having thrown off the rule of aristocratic kings a century earlier, the city and its adjacent farmlands—called Attica— now prided themselves on the electoral process.[36]

Athens' democracy was not a perfect model, however. A large percentage of its population was comprised of slaves, women, and children, and none of them had any political power whatsoever. A census recorded by Demetrius in 322 BCE estimates that slaves outnumbered Athenian citizens by 3 to 1.[37] Only free Athenian men,

---

[34] Eliot, Alexander. *The Penguin Guide to Greece.* 1991.

[35] Rostovtzeff, Mikhail. *A History of the Ancient World: The Orient and Greece.* 1926.

[36] Ibid.

[37] Cited by Hans van Wees in "Demetrius and Draco: Athens' Property Classes and Population in and Before 317 BC." *The Journal of Hellenic Studies* Vol. 131, 2011.

of whom there were about 30,000, were allowed to vote for a panel of leaders known as the archons.[38] The archons were meant to work together to discuss the issues of the day and come up with appropriate solutions that most could agree on. It was a radical method of self-governance that the Athenians were fiercely proud of.

Literature and philosophy blossomed from the relatively stable Athenian foundations, as it did in neighboring Greek cities such as Sparta and Corinth. The epic poems of Homer were taught to young male students, while complex mathematical equations and scientific theories were imparted on older boys whose parents could afford to bring in a succession of learned tutors. In some wealthy families, girls also enjoyed higher education. It was the era of the great philosopher Socrates, who believed the most important lesson a student could learn was *how* to learn. His philosophies and teaching methods created the basis for what is known as the Socratic Method, upon which most of modern Western education is based.

Ancient Hellas was home to many famous philosophers and politicians during this time, from Pericles, the great statesman, to Pythagoras, the great ascetic mathematician and religious philosopher. Thanks to an agricultural and economic system that allowed for surplus food and supplies, the cities and towns of Hellas produced great thinkers who were allowed to study with teachers for several years past the traditional age of 12. Men like Solas and Themistocles followed their subjects of interest into local politics and the military, first impressing upon Athenians the benefits of democracy and then ensuring the city was fortified against its enemies.

Celebrated as it was, Athens was not so big or powerful in the eyes of the great Persian Empire of that age. When King Xerxes came to Hellas in search of conquest in the early 5th century BCE, it was by

---

[38] Ibid.

sheer bravery and willpower that the Athenians and citizens of nearby Marathon were able to press the oncoming force back to the sea.[39] General Themistocles took the attack as a warning unto himself and his city: the military of Athens needed serious fortification. Thanks to his foresight, Athens built a lavish and immense fleet of trireme galley warships that was the envy of all Hellas.[40] Using these ships to pummel the larger Persian ships into ruin, the allied Hellenistic states defeated Xerxes in a decisive, bloody battle.

Grecian culture flourished in the centuries following that defeat, though it was structured awkwardly in a plethora of city-states, kingdoms, and temporary leagues. The northern kingdom of Macedon emerged as the most powerful of these during the reign of King Philip II from 359–336 BCE.[41] Philip used his army to force the rest of Hellas into a unified realm under his own rule which he turned over to his son Alexander upon his death in 336 BCE.[42] Better known as Alexander the Great, King Alexander of Macedon took his father's empire-building tendencies to an unprecedented level.

In just short of 13 years, Alexander's massive Greek army conquered almost the entirety of the known world, from Greece to northern India and Persia to Egypt.[43] Determined to not only bring these new countries to heel under his leadership, the conqueror also founded new cities along the way, each bearing his own name. The city of Alexandria in Egypt was one of his most revered, especially given Alexander's respect for the ancient civilization that had existed so long before his own. After fighting his way across Asia Minor, the

---

[39] Garland, Robert. *Athens Burning*. 2017.

[40] Paine, Lincoln. *The Sea and Civilization: A Maritime History of the World*. 2014.

[41] Luttenburger, Mark. *From Darius I to Phillip II: The Story of the Greek Poleis*. 2017.

[42] Ibid.

[43] Skelton, Debra and Pamela Dell. *Empire of Alexander the Great*. 2009.

Macedonian emperor was delighted to find that Egyptians welcomed him wholeheartedly into their lands, gratefully offering him the role of pharaoh after having spent many years under the subjugation of the Persian Empire. Alexandria flooded with Egyptian and Greek settlers who were eager to merge their intellectual cultures into one.

This was the pinnacle of Greek culture, where everything Alexander touched became part of his world. Educational and political systems were reorganized to mimic that of Athens, Thebes, Pella, and the other prosperous cities of Hellas. Incumbent citizens were not given a vote, however, since Alexander left his own general and political allies in charge of each new principality. Greek culture was still imprinted upon the lands of Alexander's empire, though, with the exception of Egypt, it was done so without the will of the people.

Alexander died unexpectedly at the young age of 32, leaving his massive empire in the hands of four of his generals.[44] The realms faced internal strife and competition from eastern rulers, and though each part of the empire did eventually throw off the shackles of Grecian rule, every corner of Alexander's domain retained pieces of the imposed Greek-style culture. Within Greece proper, years of civil war and leadership quarrels followed the death of the great conqueror. The civilization shrank back from the far reaches of the eastern world and tried to reorganize itself as the Achaean League in 280 BCE.[45] By 146 BCE, however, an uprising against the political intrusion of the Roman Republic caused all of Hellas to meet Rome on the battlefield.[46] The latter was the victor.

---

[44] Ibid.

[45] Wilson, Nigel. *Encyclopedia of Ancient Greece*. 2013.

[46] Ibid.

Chapter 8 – The Roman Empire

Of all the wonders that I have heard, It seems to me most strange that men should fear; Seeing death, a necessary end, Will come when it will come.

(William Shakespeare, *Julius Caesar*)

The Roman Republic was hardly a new entity in the Mediterranean. Many of its oldest cities had been founded by the Greeks and styled on the example that Athens and Hellas in general had set before it. Their civilization blossomed during the latter centuries of the Hellenistic empires and alliances, and it grew exponentially during the reign of its first emperor, Julius Caesar. Following Caesar's gruesome murder at the hands of dozens of Roman senators in 44 BCE, the republic was transformed into an empire under the rule of a dynasty of Caesar's own descendants.[47] It was that empire that unofficially stripped Greece of its monopoly over the Mediterranean and surrounding countries.

For a century, the Roman occupation of Greece was limited except in terms of collecting taxes from its Greek subjects. Athens led a failed rebellion against Rome in 88 BCE, and disorganized Roman administration of the provinces crippled the once strong economy.[48]

---

[47] Strauss, Barry. *The Death of Caesar.* 2016.

[48] Chaniotis, Angelos. *War in the Hellenistic World.* 2008.

When Rome's Emperor Augustus claimed the formal annexation of Egypt in 30 BCE, it was truly the end of the Grecian era.[49]

Emperor Augustus' reign maintained the superficial belief of Roman democracy but, in fact, turned the empire into an oligarchy. Once Greece had been subjugated, Rome became the ultimate cultural assimilator. The Senate remained, ostensibly for debate and referendums over the emperor's ideas, but only the wealthiest among the free-born Romans could be elected as representatives of the people. It was an entirely hypocritical system, one that put democracy on a pedestal while practicing aristocratic rule and dictatorship.

Regardless, the Roman Empire continued to follow in the footsteps of the Greeks in as many ways possible. One of those methods was to base most of its infrastructure and economy on slavery. Army generals and merchants from the new world power imported Greek slaves by the tens of thousands, often placing those slaves in positions of great importance to their households. Greek scholars were displaced from their homes and made to teach Roman children about philosophy, religion, mathematics, and science.

The Romans held the Greeks in as much esteem as Alexander the Great had held the Egyptians. Educated Roman politicians, administrators, and military personnel often learned their own numbers and letters at the feet of Greek tutors, and they wanted the same for their own children. The Greeks, in turn, held steadfast to their own national histories and allegiances. Tutors taught Rome's young generation all about the pantheon of Mount Olympus, which had been the crux of their spiritual and religious realm for thousands of years.

Mount Olympus is a literal peak on the border of Thessaly and Macedonia where ancient Greeks believed all the gods and goddesses

---

[49] Carratelli, Giovanni Pugliese. *Roma e l'Egitto.* 1992.

of their universe lived in splendor.[50] There was Zeus, the great warrior with his magical lightning; Athena, goddess of war, dressed for battle; and dozens of other mythological figures who graced the pages of Greek histories and acted as real characters in Homer's stories of the Trojan War. The pantheon lived on in the Roman Republic, though the names of the deities were transformed. Zeus became Jupiter; Athena became Diana. It was simultaneously the eradication of Greek culture and the assimilation of it.

While they used the Greeks to educate their children, aristocratic citizens of the Roman Empire were free to focus on their own personal satisfaction. Slaves danced, sang, played musical instruments like the lute, and fed their captors, while others acted in stage plays alongside free men. There was no end to all the lavish luxuries a full citizen of Rome could enjoy: feasts of the finest imported foods, gladiatorial combat shows, dinner parties, wine parties, story-telling bards, poetry, libraries—even executions were events the public attended and enjoyed. Of course, this was not the case for Roman women or foreign-born men, neither of whom had dominion over their own lives and choices. The Roman Empire was a world controlled by Roman men, with very few exceptions.

At its peak, the empire included all the land that stretched from Britannia (the Roman name for Britain) and all of Western Europe to Mauritania and along the coast of North Africa to Egypt, as well as around the eastern rim of the Mediterranean Sea to encapsulate Saudi Arabia, Syria, and Babylon. The latter was renamed Constantinople by Emperor Constantine in 330 CE.[51] With so many resources available to its emperors and wealthy citizens, the Roman Empire built a vast and highly structured civilization. Marble from Italy was shipped to Britannia to establish the new city of Londinium, which

---

[50] Shea, John. *Macedonia and Greece: The Struggle.* 2016.

[51] Anderson, Zachary. *The Fall of Rome and the Rise of Constantinople.* 2015.

followed the planning style of Rome itself. Indeed, each new city of the empire was constructed with its main temples and amphitheater at its heart with a collection of rectangular clusters of shops, public buildings, and homes radiating outward.

Londinium (later called London) had a rocky start thanks to the repeated attacks of native tribes, but its founders persevered. It, along with Colonia Agrippina (Cologne), Vindobona (Vienna), Nida (Frankfurt), and Aquincum (Budapest), survived into the modern age thanks to Rome's finely tuned systems of road construction, concrete mixing, mathematically sound architecture, and cultural oppression. Just as Alexander the Great had conquered the Eastern European realms a few centuries before, Rome's emperors did the same with their focus in the opposite direction. They implanted Roman culture into almost the entire European continent through the most vulnerable and willing members of local societies: the children.

Children of wealthy and important families in newly conquered Roman provinces were very important to the future of the realm. Their families were usually given advantages if they survived the conquest. It was in an emperor's best interests to make allies quickly in conquered lands, and it was easiest to do so by offering positions of authority to those who had been in charge of the previous administration. This way, local polities didn't collapse outright. Powerful men remained so, and their children were schooled in the way of the Romans. It was a plan in which the youth of the provinces grew up viewing the empire as the reason for his continued life of luxury and impressive education. Of course, they were quickly indoctrinated with Roman political and philosophical propaganda.

Rome's objective greatness started to sink following the death of Emperor Constantine. He was the first to accept the new Christian religion, and in doing so, he set events in motion that would completely change the face of European religious history. Before Christianity came to benefit Rome, however, emperors struggled for nearly two centuries to manage an overwhelmingly large realm that ultimately split in two.

Despite the fall of the Western Roman Empire, their educational system (copied from the Greeks) permanently imprinted the idea of the Roman Empire as a gilded distributor of enlightenment, knowledge, and democracy upon the students of its vast realm. While they did indeed spread the teachings of famed philosophers and scientists, of literate leaders and political theologists, Rome also managed to export the idea that strong economies were founded on slavery. Though direct slavery would fade alongside the glory of the empire, its premise was reconstructed in post-Roman Europe.

Chapter 9 – The Vikings

The sky rests on the shoulders of four dwarfs. They stand at its corners, holding it up, and their names are Nordri, Sudri, Ostri and Westri...

(Henry Myers, *The Utmost Island*)

The northern realm was not empty and silent while the rest of Europe busied itself in the business of its neighbors near and far. Though the climate was considerably harsher than that of the Mediterranean, humanity flourished all the same. The Danes, as they were wont to call themselves at that time, grew oats, barley, rye, and grass, the latter to feed their livestock. In vegetable gardens, households grew turnips, beans, peas, and carrots, all of which were traditionally boiled with cuts of meat to form a thick, hearty stew. All in all, the diet and daily work of an ancient Dane was remarkably similar to that of a modern farmer.

For several millennia, the Danes had neither the means nor the desire to leave their farms or small communities in search of distant shores. Their time was precious, and most fishing boats were too small to bear more than a pair of people past the point at which the shoreline disappeared from sight. These were boats powered entirely by paddles and had limited strength and speed. Early Vikings were satisfied with the canoes that helped them catch seemingly unlimited quantities of codfish, just as they were content with a loaf of bread and a bowl of meaty stew for supper.

In the early Middle Ages, at least three Scandinavian towns existed by the 8th century CE.[52] One such town was Hedeby, found in the northernmost part of modern Germany. Situated near the eastern shore of the Kattegat, into which the Baltic Sea drains, Hedeby was probably reorganized by merchants who'd been forced to flee the destroyed trading center of Reric on the coast of the Baltic. It became a vital trading city, especially since the Vikings had just made big strides in maritime transportation.

Scandinavia's coastal people had finally perfected the longship: a light and graceful craft about 30 meters (98 feet) in length with space to fit as many as 100 men and women.[53] About sixty of the longship's occupants were tasked with rowing, while a square sail was positioned to catch a favorable wind. The combined strength of the rowers and wind allowed Danish sailors to travel up to 15 knots per hour, covering long distances in a reasonably short amount of time. The big boats also provided a higher degree of protection than their smaller predecessors did, which gave sailing crews the confidence to set out for distant shores both known and unknown.

Curious fishermen and farmers commissioned such longships of their own and piloted these across the Baltic to meet with other groups of Danes. They brought warm furs and slaves to trade with the communities they found throughout Scandinavia and eventually those located throughout Eastern Europe. Popular Scandinavian items included soapstone bowls and cooking pots, whetstones for sharpening tools, and iron ore. In exchange, the Vikings brought home glass and ceramics, cloth, salt, wine, tin, and copper. It was a remarkable era for the Vikings whose entire world was suddenly opened up and put within reach. In Hedeby, the population boomed.

---

[52] Bairoch, P. *Cities and Economic Development: From the Dawn of History to the Present.* 1988.

[53] Chartrand, Rene; Durham, Keith; and Mark Harrison. *The Vikings.* 2016.

Craftsmen, merchants, and youth in search of employment crowded into the city to send their wares off on ships and excitedly search through new shipments from exotic lands. This import and export business characterized much of the next two centuries, though farming, fishing, and animal husbandry remained at the heart of Norse culture.

By the 10th century, Viking kings and their sailors were quite familiar with the world around them.[54] They'd visited Constantinople, traded with the Islamic caliphate, and even set foot in the lands of the Slavs (modern Russia). Adventurous Vikings had founded new towns across Scandinavia to facilitate more trading, both domestic and international. A Viking settlement was even founded in Dublin, Ireland, to better compete with the well-established partnerships between the British Isles and the European mainland.

This Dublin trading hub would serve the native Irish well since trade with Britannia soon grew out of fashion with the Norsemen. The Vikings were delighted by the riches of Europe, but by comparison, they had little to trade. Furs and slaves were in demand, but there were only so many that could be obtained each season, and arable land had started to run short in Scandinavia. The growing population of Vikings put a serious strain on the northern part of the continent, and without much room to start new farms or harvest more food, the leaders of the northern people overhauled their economic system. Tribes and cities without fortifications and the protection of a king's army became targets for fearsome raiding parties.

The 800s, 900s, and 1000s saw countless violent raids.[55] The Vikings attacked small neighbors, distant economic rivals, and generally any settlements that were not protected enough to offer any sort of

---

[54] Ciggaar, K.N. *Western Travellers to Constantinople: The West and Byzantium.* 1996.

[55] Grant, R.G. *Warrior: A Visual History of the Fighting Man.* 2007.

retaliation. Viking families and tribes banded together in raiding parties, sailing east or west to strike unsuspecting communities and plunder their treasures. The raiders ran in, brandishing axes, hammers, and daggers, and murdered their way into the heart of each town. Once the local population was mostly dead or at least subdued in bonds, the raiders seized everything of value, from silver goblets and animals to women and men. Both sexes became slaves, either in the form of a wife, a laborer, or both.

Hungry for treasure and land, thousands of Vikings sailed into Britannia to sack and plunder the precious metals of the Christian churches they found there. Unable to sack Paris, the Norsemen were offered a piece of land in the Frankish kingdom in exchange for their loyalty to the Frankish King Charles the Simple. The land was settled by the Viking leader Rollo and his followers as the Duchy of Normandy in 911 CE.[56] At the very end of that same century, the Viking civilization of mainland Europe had reached such peaks that its population spilled over the edges and began to search for new worlds. Iceland, Greenland, and Canada all felt the heavy weight of the Viking longships running aground before the turn of the millennium. These Arctic landmasses were a few degrees warmer around the year 1000 CE, which made them perfect sites for families in search of new beginnings.[57]

Though Vikings would always pride themselves on their physical strength and achievements in warfare, they wanted their own land to farm alongside their families. These new islands provided an opportunity to do just that. Raiding fell away again as settlers found the space to spread out comfortably and turn the soil, just as their ancestors had done in Scandinavia. They brought their pantheon with

---

[56] McKay, John P; Hill, Bennett D; and John Buckler. *A History of Western Society.* 2002.

[57] Richard, Kenneth. "Arctic Was Warmer 9,000 Years Ago When C02 was Low." *Principia Scientific International.* 16 July 2018.

them and were sure to make the necessary sacrifices to the gods Thor, Odin, Freya, and their kin. Truly, theirs was the last stand of ancestral religion in Europe and the colonies. The Norsemen of the mainland abandoned the raids when enemy armies proved too great to overcome and became inundated with the new religion of the era, Christianity. In L'Anse aux Meadows in Newfoundland, settlers lost faith in the old gods when they failed to provide enough colonists and supplies from home to support the settlement. Slowly, the Danes trickled back to Greenland and then out of the New World altogether.

The era of gruesome Viking raids with wooden statues of Thor perched at the bow of great longships ended; Christianity painted over it to match the rest of the continent.

Chapter 10 – The Dark Ages

Very often it has come to my mind what men of learning there were formerly throughout England, both in religious and secular orders; and how there were happy times then throughout England… and how nowadays, if we wished to acquire these things, we would have to seek them outside.

(King Alfred of Wessex, *Pastoral Care*)

As Rome's soldiers, builders, politicians, teachers, craftsmen, and merchants slowly made their exit from the western reaches of the empire as the Western Roman Empire fell, whole nations of people were left uncertain of their futures. The previously laid infrastructures of Britannia, Brittany, and other western lands fell into disrepair without imported materials flooding the region. The architects and city leaders left behind had the knowledge of roadbuilding, fortification, maintenance, and overseas trade, but due to a population crash, there was little time for anything except farming, animal husbandry, gardening, and food preparation. The great pursuits of the Roman Empire, such as education, literature, and the arts, were abandoned for more pressing activities. As the decades and centuries marched on, Roman culture became a distant memory.

There was a deeply divided group of people left in Britannia: People who considered themselves blooded members of Roman families and those who felt more kinship to the Celtic and Druid traditions of the past. Those who had been part of Roman families or worked alongside the aristocrats of Rome believed that they must do whatever possible to maintain the culture of their late administrators and masters. On the other side of the divide were the people whose lands had been stolen, whose villages had been burned, and whose families had starved to serve the excesses of the Roman Empire. The native tribes of Britannia celebrated their freedom from distant Rome and made haste to reintroduce their own cultures to lands that had been without them for centuries.

Throughout Western Europe, it was much the same. Gaul, whose territory began at the far western edge of the mainland, was divided up among the Visigoths, the Burgundians, and the Franks when Rome's soldiers retreated to Italy. When the Gauls successfully routed the remaining governors of the empire in 486 CE, they established their own monarchal rule under the leadership of Merovich.[58] It was the first move toward unifying all of the Celtic Gauls. Two generations later, under Merovich's grandson, Clovis I, all of Gaul was united at the tip of the sword into the Kingdom of the Franks. Theirs was the Merovingian Dynasty, and it grew to encompass the fallen Western Roman Empire and much of Alemannia (modern Germany).

The Frankish kingdom inherited a sense of superiority not only from its military prowess but from the fact that it had annexed part of the former Roman seat of power. The Merovingians felt they had earned the right and responsibility to establish a new age in which they, the French, dictated the rest of the continent. To this end, Clovis I found it both logical and tactically necessary to become a Christian.[59] His conversion was recorded in *The Chronicle of St. Denis*, which

---

[58] Waldman, C. and Mason C. *Encyclopedia of European Peoples.* 2006

[59] Iyigun, M. *War, Peace, and Prosperity in the Name of God.* 2015.

explains how he called upon the Christian God as a last resort in beating the Alemannia people in battle and gaining their lands for his own:

At this time the King was yet in the errors of his idolatry and went to war with the Alemanni, since he wished to render them tributary. Long was the battle, many were slain on one side or the other, for the Franks fought to win glory and renown, the Alemanni to save life and freedom. When the King at length saw the slaughter of his people and the boldness of his foes, he had greater expectation of disaster than of victory. He looked up to heaven humbly, and spoke thus: "Most mighty God, whom my queen Clothilde worships and adores with heart and soul, I pledge you perpetual service unto your faith, if only you give me now the victory over my enemies."

Instantly when he had said this, his men were filled with burning valor, and a great fear smote his enemies, so that they turned their backs and fled the battle; and victory remained with the King and with the Franks. The king of the Alemanni were slain; and as for the Alemanni, seeing themselves discomfited, and that their king had fallen, they yielded themselves to Chlodovocar and his Franks and became his tributaries.

The King returned after this victory into Frankland. He went to Rheims, and told the Queen what had befallen; and they together gave thanks unto Our Lord.

Queen Clotilde's influence on this decision—or rather, this outburst—is clear. She was already a devout Christian, one of the few such people in Western Europe at the time. It was possibly a sense of reverence for the importance of the old Roman Empire, which had embraced Christianity in the latter centuries of its rule, that enticed the royal couple to consider adopting the relatively new religion for their empire. Thenceforth, the official religion of the Franks was Roman Catholicism. King Clovis I was baptized on Christmas Day of 508 CE.

The Frankish kingdom was not the only one to establish itself firmly in the absence of the Western Roman Empire. The Iberian Peninsula was ruled by the Visigoths; the northern countries by the Danes, Jutes, Saxons, and Frisians; and the remnants of the Roman Empire still held its own throughout Greece, Egypt, and Persia. Mostly unconcerned with the goings-on of Europe, however, the Asian-facing Eastern Roman Empire soon came under a rebranded moniker: The Byzantine Empire. The Kingdom of Odoacer filled the political vacuum in Italy, thereby preserving the realm in its original physical state if not in its original administrative structure. At the far eastern stretches of Europe lay the Kingdoms of the Rugii, the Ostrogoths, and the Nepos.

Many philosophers and historians of the Middle Ages would refer to this crucial period as the Dark Ages as a metaphor for the lost light of the highly educated, modern Roman Empire. Despite the moniker, the years 500-1000 BCE were not characteristic of a decline in intelligence, nor were they a time of crisis for the people of post-Roman Europe.[60] Certainly, there were difficulties given the collapse of such a vast economic network, but for many of the oppressed and suppressed cultures of Europe, the collapse of Classical Rome signaled the beginning of an era of local authority. The traditions of the Celts, Druids, Visigoths, Alemanni, and others had the chance to practice again and establish their own terms with neighboring European realms.

While Europe found its feet and explored its own potential, Rome struggled to do the same. Back in the Italian Peninsula, the surviving section of the Roman Empire was busy rebranding itself into a new, Middle-Age-friendly version of its old colonial self. The transformation's key player was a Frankish king known as Charles the Great. King Charles, or Charles le Magne in his own tongue, united the Frankish realm with that of Northern Italy and Germany. Pope Leo III crowned Charlemagne—as he is now known to history—Emperor

---

[60] Demid, David. *Science and Technology in World History.* 2014.

of the Romans on Christmas Day of the year 800 CE.[61] Since Irene of Athens had named herself the Roman emperor in place of her son, Constantine VI, there were henceforth two Emperors of Rome. Charlemagne ruled the western portion, and Irene and her successors the east. Soon, the divided empire became known as the Holy Roman Empire in the west and the Byzantine Empire in the east.

While the Byzantines centered their realm in Constantinople and used the Greek language, Charlemagne ruled his Latin empire from Aachen in modern-day Germany. Both were established as Christian entities, but it was the western empire that would become permanently fixed as the world's capital of Catholicism.

---

[61] Curta, F. and Holt, A. – Editors., *Great Events in Religion - Encyclopedia of Pivotal Events in Religious History.* 2017.

Chapter 11 – The Holy Roman Empire

The Holy Roman Empire is neither Holy, nor Roman, nor an Empire.

(Voltaire)

The once proud and great city of Rome came under attack by the Ostrogoths in the mid-5th century CE and was ravaged to ruin.[62] Under the instructions of Bessus, the general of the Eastern Roman Empire in charge of its former capital, citizens were prohibited from leaving Rome during the year-long siege of the city. Starving, the workers and farmers of the empire—called "plebeians"—resorted to eating dogs, rodents, wild greens, and the low-calorie remnants left behind from the filtered white flour of the wealthy.[63] People wasted away from hunger and died in the streets. By the time they were allowed to leave, many died on the way to find help.

The Ostrogoth ruler, King Totila, succeeded in destroying the final Roman ranks and proceeded to tear down most of the city's defensive walls. Everyone fled, leaving no more than a few hundred people within the opened gates. Despite an attempt to rebuild the very next

---

[62] Davis, P.K. *Besieged: 100 Great Sieges from Jericho to Sarajevo.* 2003.

[63] Bury, J.B. "History of the Later Roman Empire." *Macmillan & Co. Ltd.* 1923.

year, Totila's forces kept up the pressure and retook the city in 549 CE.[64] Afterward, he decided to repopulate the city himself, establishing a guard there to protect it against the counterattacks of the Roman-born Byzantine Emperor Justinian I.

The next three centuries went by in a similar fashion, though a succession of Byzantine emperors claimed true ownership over the ancient city. They conducted their business in Constantinople, however, and did not deign to spend much time in Rome except to erect statues and impart their importance on the citizens there. By the 7th century CE, Italy had decisively come under the administration of the Alemanni and the Franks, due to the fact that the Byzantine Empire was facing a slew of enemies on its home front.[65] Despite all of them being Christian nations, they nevertheless did not hesitate to inflict war upon one another for gains in wealth or land.

The Christian age was ironically no more peaceful or less warlike for its newfound faith in the Catholic Church. The devoutly Christian King of the Franks, Charles the Great—or Charlemagne, as he became known—conducted a long military campaign against the Lombard Kingdom in the latter part of the 8th century.[66] The Lombards' authority held in the region surrounding Rome, as well as in Sicily, Sardinia, and the far southern parts of mainland Italy. Charlemagne's venture was ultimately successful with the lands being handed over to the papacy in exchange for the lives of the royal family.

Italy and the newly conquered Rome maintained strong ties to the Roman Catholic Church and the papacy. Built upon the tradition of Frankish Catholicism that had been in place since Clovis I,

---

[64] Hodgkin, T. *Italy and Her Invaders: 553-600. Book VI.* Web.

[65] Kleinhenz, C. *Routledge Revivals: Medieval Italy (2004): An Encyclopedia -, Volume 2.* 2004.

[66] Bachrach, B. *Charlemagne's Early Campaigns (768-777): A Diplomatic and Military Analysis.* 2013.

Charlemagne worked ferociously to knit together a kingdom that was purely Christian. In the year 800 CE, reigning Pope Leo III personally took the future of Italy in his own hands when he selected King Charles to rule as Holy Roman Emperor.[67]

This was a clever move designed not only for self-protection and the consolidation of authority but to also rebel against the rule of a female on the Byzantine throne. The Byzantine Emperor Irene of Athens was unable to defend her own dynastic claim to the land because of ongoing political strife and revolt. Unchallenged, Charlemagne accepted his new territory of Northern Italy and most of Germany, Austria, Switzerland, and Poland under its newly delineated borders.

Charlemagne kept the Kingdom of the Franks isolated and independent under its own domain, probably because rulership over the Holy Roman Empire was subject to the will of the Pope and not any particular family dynasty. The two realms were closely connected, however, and together they formed the vast majority of the continent. From this foundation, Catholicism was established as the most influential and important religion of medieval Europe. Charlemagne had been ordained by God's own messenger, or so he believed, to rule the land, and by that same power, his own sons and their sons would take on the Kingdom of the Franks after his death.

For monarchs during this period of European history, religion became the logical reason for why they imparted their power and supposed wisdom on their subjects; it was also the reason given for dynastic rule. No matter what befell a Catholic king, be it assassination, kidnapping, or usurpation, his people were compelled to replace him with a successor of the same lineage. Wealth, lands, and authority were forever to be maintained in the hands of one family, as chosen by God himself. The civilians were taught by their church leaders to

---

[67] Sypeck, J. *Becoming Charlemagne: Europe, Baghdad, and the Empires of A.D. 800.* 2006.

respect and almost worship their kings as God's representatives. Punishment for ignoring this indoctrination or speaking against it was harsh and usually culminated in death.

Though it was internally fragmented, the Holy Roman Empire was politically arranged so that its main export was Catholicism and, therefore, power. The assemblage of the Pope, the Holy Roman Empire, and the King of Franks worked together to simultaneously teach their citizens the laws of Christianity and impart a sense of ultimate authority. Immense and ornate Catholic churches were built throughout the realm in which bishops and priests were appointed to provide services for the public. Lateran Palace, in Rome, underwent lavish refurbishments so that it could serve as the permanent home of the Pope.[68] The rulers of the land spared no expense in creating an awe-inspiring Catholic domain, the likes of which most people had never seen.

Rome, Italy, and the rest of Europe had most definitively recovered from the collapse of the original Roman Empire, though everything looked quite different than it had just 500 years previously. With the Catholic Pope at home in rebuilt Rome and most of Europe under the administration of monarchs with unprecedented wealth, power, and military strength, the continent's farmers, craftsmen, workers, and families refocused their capabilities on serving one god. Catholic Europe strode confidently into the Middle Ages.

---

[68] Thunø, E. *Image and Relic: Mediating the Sacred in Early Medieval Rome*. 2002.

Chapter 12 – The Rise of Wessex

For in prosperity a man is often puffed up with pride, whereas tribulations chasten and humble him through suffering and sorrow. In the midst of prosperity the mind is elated, and in prosperity a man forgets himself...

(King Alfred, *The Anglo-Saxon Chronicle*)

In former Britannia, Germanic migration had had a big effect on the cultural and linguistic makeup of the land. Celtic peoples, Latins, and Germanic tribes intermingled so completely in many parts of Britain that the largest cultural body was soon a mixture of all the existing lifestyles. Proto-English became tied into the Germanic languages, and the people of Britain came to identify themselves as Anglo-Saxons: that is, Germanic peoples living in England. Anglo-Saxon culture dominated Britain as early as the 5th century CE,[69] and it was these people who established a number of small kingdoms throughout England.

Each of these domains was headed by a dictatorial monarch who used the power of his army to sustain local law and defend against the attacks of his fellow kings. The monarchs faced the most political and military opposition from their neighbors, and though each attempted in his turn to make peace agreements and alliances, ultimately, the fate of the kingdoms fell to the warcraft of its soldiers.

---

[69] Sanders, R.H. and Sanders, R. *German: Biography of a Language*. 2010.

After a few centuries of royal marriages between kingdoms and warfare between the regions, Wessex overtook its neighbors as the largest, most highly populated, and most influential kingdom of all Britain. The others consolidated themselves into Mercia, Northumbria, and East Anglia. In 925 CE, King Athelstan stood at the head of all but one of these: Northumbria.[70] A pious and deeply Catholic man, Athelstan believed it was his duty to unite the English kingdoms under one crown and see to their religious upbringing. The last holdout to his plan was York, a Northumbrian realm under Viking control.

The Viking presence in Britannia had been in place for centuries by that point, and Athelstan's own royal ancestors had spent a great deal of their own reigns dealing with them in a multitude of ways. The Danish raids had by no means ceased, but some of their farmers had been given land to work in exchange for peace. Treaties had been repeatedly broken on both sides, and King Athelstan had no qualms about turning his army toward York to eradicate them completely from his burgeoning, united kingdom. First, however, he used the age-old tradition of marrying his sister to its Viking king.

When King Sihtric married Athelstan's sister, he made an agreement with Athelstan that neither of them would wage war on the other or support one another's enemies. The treaty was kept all of one year as Sihtric died in 927, and Athelstan quickly ushered in his troops in support of his sister, the acting queen.[71] His campaign was successful, resulting in total kingship over the kingdoms of England and the political clout to cow the kings of Wales to his will. The Kingdom of Scots and the Kingdom of Strathclyde officially recognized Athelstan as the ruler of their close geographical neighbor, Northumberland, as

---

[70] Giles, J.A. and Ingram, J. *The Anglo-Saxon Chronicle: A Collaborative Edition.* Web.

[71] Palliser, D. M. *Medieval York: 600-1540.* 2014.

well as the multiple kingdoms to the south. Athelstan established the Welsh lands as polities under his own leadership and became the first King of all England.[72]

There was much work to do for King Athelstan, and he set to it immediately. First, he appointed men he trusted to administer the counties and annexed kingdoms and see to it that any revolts were quickly curbed. Next, he saw to it that the weights of currency were regulated and that fraudsters were strictly penalized for creating coins of false silver or gold. He also reinvigorated the market sector of his country by encouraging all trade to take place within fortified spaces, thereby making buyers and sellers much safer from thieves or raiders. This move took many people from rural homes into the urban centers of England, where trade and craftsmanship increased simultaneously.

Urbanization and agriculture were both necessary elements of the Anglo-Saxons under King Athelstan's power. Towns were essential for merchantry and religious ceremonies, while agriculture remained fundamental to the civilization. True to his word, Athelstan funded existing Catholic churches throughout his kingdom and founded many more. Wessex, already heavily marked by the stone henges, barrows, and man-made hills of the Celts, became dotted with majestic cathedrals. The Malmesbury Cathedral in modern Wiltshire was a favorite of King Athelstan, who frequented it for services and made regular donations there.

Wessex remained the seat of power in England for the duration of the Middle Ages, and the importance the king put on religious education and faith had a lasting impact there. London, having survived the withdrawal of the Romans who founded it, prospered at the apex of European trade through the English Channel. King Athelstan encouraged international commerce and positive relationships by having the female members of his family marry into important

---

[72] Foot, S. *AEthelstan*. 2011.

families of mainland Europe.

At home, a strict hierarchy of social classes was maintained, with the Royal House of Wessex at the top and a multitude of serfs at the bottom.[73] It was the same as in the rest of ancient Europe with indentured servants providing the virtually free labor necessary to support a growing economy and political realm. The work of Athelstan, his administrators, the nobility, the free people, and the serfs of the 10th century were immeasurable in its value to contemporary and future Britain—even despite the hardships it was about to face.

---

[73] Piggott, S. and Thirsk, J. – Editors. *The Agrarian History of England and Wales: Volume 1, Part 1, Prehistory.* 1981.

Chapter 13 – The Norman Conquest

If we had to sum this new society up in a single word, we might describe it as feudal— but only if we were prepared for an outbreak of fainting fits among medieval historians .

(Marc Morris, *The Norman Conquest: The Battle of Hastings and the Fall of Anglo-Saxon England*)

Even the Vikings had entered the Christian Age, albeit slowly and without adhering strictly to the tenets laid down by Rome. Their intrepid counterparts in Normandy—a small Frankish realm on the southern coast of the English Channel—had done so as well, perhaps more willingly than their ancestors up north. By the 11th century CE, the Normans were Francophone Christians, but they had by no means given up their ancient tradition of plundering and conquering.[74]

In 1028 CE, a descendant of Rollo, the first Viking-Norman chief, was born to Robert I, Duke of Normandy.[75] Illegitimate though he was, that boy, William, succeeded his father as the next Duke of Normandy

---

[74] Miller, C. and Miller, J. *War: History and Philosophy of War.* 2017.

[75] Cawthorne, Nigel. *Kings & Queens of England.* 2009.

in childhood.[76] Several members of the royal family argued over who should rule in place of William, but ultimately, thanks to the fact that the young duke had the support of the public, he remained in power into his adulthood.

Since the Duchy of Normandy was still answerable to the Kingdom of the Franks, William's power ended at the borders—and that wasn't good enough for him. Realizing he would need more political clout to stay in power and thrive, the duke married Matilda of Flanders, heiress of a neighboring Dutch realm. Assembling an army with the help of his wife's family, William wrested control of Normandy from the Franks. Soon afterward, he annexed the County of Maine as well.[77]

Due to his royal heritage—legitimate or not—William of Normandy could link his familial roots to the English throne. Across the English Channel, King Edward the Confessor had died following a rebellion and subsequent banishment from his own court. Childless, the English throne could only fall to one of two main candidates, both of whom were related to Edward. The first was Harold of Godwinson, Earl of Wessex and Hereford. The second was William of Normandy. Although William claimed Edward had promised the crown to him, Harold was crowned immediately upon Edward's death in January of 1066.[78]

William had no intentions to bow to Harold as the King of England, and he knew that according to the law of the land he had the necessary bloodline to rule. Determined to take Harold's throne, William put together an army and a fleet of ships and made for England. He was not the only one to do so; Tostig, brother of Godwinson, and King

---

[76] Cawthorne, N. *Kings & Queens of England.* 2011.

[77] Evensen, S.T. *The Altruistic Gene - Revisited: About Actions, Events and Impacts.* 2019.

[78] Grossman, M. *World Military Leaders: A Biographical Dictionary.* 2007.

Harald III of Norway were also vying for the throne. In September of 1066, each contender marched on Britannia.[79]

Godwinson was prepared. He defeated both his brother and Harald III at the Battle of Stamford Bridge on September 25. With both potential usurpers killed in the fight, only William remained a contender for the crown. He moved in confidently, landing his fleet at Pevensey in the south of England. There, he made his base camp. King Harold marched south to meet the invaders and was met by his enemy just north of Hastings, some 17.7 kilometers (11 miles) up the coast from William's original camp on the beach. It was October 14 when the two sides engaged in a 12-hour battle from morning to dusk.

Fighting with about 8,000 troops, mostly infantrymen, against William's collection of about 10,000 fighters comprised of cavalrymen, archers, and infantrymen, King Harold found himself at a disadvantage.[80] Repeatedly, he seemed to have the upper hand as William's troops fled the battlefield in terror, but this proved only to be a battle tactic. The Normans were only pretending to run away in an attempt to goad the English into pursuing them and thereby breaking their powerful shield wall. These tactics were not particularly successful, but William's forces still had the advantage. Early in the evening, King Harold was slain, and soon afterward, the battle was over.[81]

William the Conqueror, as he is more commonly known to modern readers, was crowned King of England on Christmas Day of 1066, and though his rule was not undisputed, it did persevere. Ruling under the title King William I, William had dozens of castles built throughout

---

[79] Marren, P. *1066: The Battles of York, Stamford Bridge & Hastings*. Web.

[80] Powell, John. *Magill's Guide to Military History*. 2001.

[81] Ibid.

his new lands, including the famous Tower of London.[82] Much like the Iron Age Britons, these castles were built on hilltops and surrounded with a ditch and a ringed hill for fortification.

William was not just the first Norman King of England; he was also the man responsible for the end of Anglo-Saxon rule over all the unified realms of Wessex, Mercia, Northumbria, and East Anglia. This was a major political and cultural shift during which a variety of French customs were imparted upon the conquered people. William and his court, as well as the new aristocratic class of Normans, spoke French and recorded their official documents the same way. A hierarchy appeared between Anglophones and Francophones, with the latter on the wealthier, more influential side.

William did not change much of the local administrative system he'd taken from the Anglo-Saxons, instead simply sending his own people to cover existing posts.[83] The Normans were now in charge of everything from collecting taxes to presiding over the English courts. William confiscated lands from all the English nobility who had fought with King Harold and redistributed them to his own Norman nobles. In an attempt to fully infiltrate England with a relatively small number of Normans, he split up the noble landholdings throughout the country instead of concentrating each noble's holdings in one large block.[84] As for the wealthy English families who remained, William arranged for their sons and daughters to marry Normans. By encouraging such marriages, King William I ensured that future generations living in England could trace their heritage both to the Anglo-Saxon culture and the Norman culture.

---

[82] Morris, M. *Castles: Their History and Evolution in Medieval Britain.* Web.

[83] Kishlansky, M.A., Geary, P.J., O'Brien, P. *Civilization in the West, Volume 1.* 2001.

[84] Paxton, Jennifer Ph.D. "The Story of Medieval England: From King Arthur to the Tudor Conquest." *THE GREAT COURSES.* 2010.

The most incredible piece of documentation from William's English rule is *The Domesday Book*, in which each county of England was listed and accompanied by a painstaking inventory of every single animal, barrel of grain, house, and item of value.[85] The king commissioned this massive document—which is still in existence today—in order to determine what he should expect to earn in taxes from each county, as well as to list all the debts that had been owed to the previous king.

As a result of the Norman Conquest, thousands of English nobles fled to Ireland, Scotland, Scandinavia, and the Byzantine Empire, establishing a scattering of settlements known as New London and New York. The farmers and laborers, with no means to undertake such expensive journeys, remained and were caught up in the new king's feudal system. Becoming indentured servants of the Crown, England's poor were put to work creating food for William's court in exchange for the right to live on the king's lands and keep enough food for their own use. Formal slavery, on the other hand, experienced a deep decline.

William I was succeeded on the English throne by his son, William II; he was followed by his brother, Henry I. Henry, in turn, was meant to be succeeded by his daughter, Empress Matilda. The throne was usurped by Henry's nephew Stephen of Blois, however, and thereafter, the feud between Matilda and Stephen threw England into a civil war.[86] Matilda's son, Henry of Anjou, was named Stephen's successor thanks to intervention from the Catholic Church, and he became King Henry II of England in 1154.[87] He founded the long-lived Plantagenet dynasty. During the rule of the Plantagenets,

---

[85] Darby, H.C. *Domesday England.* 1977.

[86] "Stephen and Matilda." *Royal.uk.* Web.

[87] "Henry II 'Curtmantle.'" *Royal.uk.* Web.

England's courts and aristocracy phased out the use of French, though it had already mixed a great deal with the Anglo-Saxon language to form Middle English.

The Plantagenets took England into the Middle Ages to mingle with Ireland, Wales, Scotland, the Kingdom of the Franks, and its most revered ally, the Holy Roman Empire. Big changes were coming once more, and this time, they began in Italy.

Chapter 14 – Marco Polo and Renaissance Italy

You know what the fellow said – in Italy, for thirty years under the Borgias, they had warfare, terror, murder and bloodshed, but they produced Michelangelo, Leonardo da Vinci and the Renaissance. In Switzerland, they had brotherly love, they had five hundred years of democracy and peace – and what did that produce? The cuckoo clock.

(Graham Greene, *The Third Man*)

The Renaissance, as proposed by Western historians, is the period of history that prominently follows the European Dark Ages. First used in the 18th century, the term "Renaissance" means "rebirth" in French.[88] This rebirth refers to a conscious return to the ideas and methodology of Classical Antiquity—that is, the Greeks and Romans, on whom many of Europe's 13th- to 16th-century population was fixated. Similar to Classical Antiquity, the Renaissance classicists first appeared in the Mediterranean. The Republic of Florence and the Republic of Venice were at the forefront of this movement.

One of the countless wonderful products of Renaissance Venice was a man called Marco Polo. Born in 1254 to a merchant family, Marco Polo learned the importance and art of importing and exporting from

---

[88] Thackeray, Frank W. and John. E. Findling (editors.) *Events that Changed the World Through the Sixteenth Century.* 2001.

his father and uncle, Niccolò and Maffeo.[89] The family traveled extensively to procure rare, in-demand items throughout West Asia that they could sell profitably back in Venice. The Silk Road beckoned to them strongly, and most of their years were spent traversing Asia and conducting trade within the exotic realms of India, Asia Minor, Mongolia, and China. Tea, gold, pearls, drugs, ivory, spices, jewels, and, of course, silk textiles were their products of choice, just as valuable in Asia as they were in Europe.[90]

At the court of Kublai Khan, the leader of the Mongols of Central Asia, Marco Polo found extravagance and luxury that he had not expected. To Westerners, the Mongols were considered a barbaric and bloodthirsty people; at court, however, the Polos learned their prejudice was unfounded. Like kings of the West, Kublai Khan lived in architectural splendor, surrounded by beautiful and ornate objects of great monetary value. At the Khan's capital city of Cambaluc, the walls were covered in gold and silver, and the dining hall could host 6,000 guests.[91] Thousands of lions, leopards, wild boars, and elephants roamed the grounds. Said Marco Polo of the city and its many rhinoceros: "They have wild elephants, and plenty of unicorns, which are scarcely smaller than elephants."[92]

Kublai Khan greatly valued knowledge of the world outside his realm, and he found the merchant Polo family to be an endless source of information and entertainment. He insisted they stay at court with him, which the whole family did for a time, even moving with the entire court from Shangdu to Cambaluc. The family business was revered above all else for the patriarchal Polos, however, and before long,

---

[89] Zelenyj, Alexander. *Marco Polo: Overland to China*. 2006.

[90] Hanif Raza, M. *A Souvenir of KKH, Gilgit, Hunza & Skardu: Saga of Silk Route.* 1996.

[91] MacFarquhar, Roderick. *The Forbidden City*. 1972.

[92] Polo, Marco. Cited in Alexander Zelenyj's *Marco Polo: Overland to China*. 2006.

Marco's uncle and father decided to move on. They saw young Marco's desire to stay behind with the Khan as a welcome way to remain in Kublai Khan's good graces. Niccolò and Maffeo returned to business traveling throughout Asia, leaving Marco at the Khan's court among thousands of other servants and administrators.[93]

Marco Polo spent more than two decades with the Mongols.[94] Having earned the trust of the mighty Khan, Polo had the ability to travel extensively throughout Mongol territory on administrative duties that might have included tax collection and even the governorship of Hangzhou, a Chinese city annexed under the rule of Kublai Khan.[95] He was the first European to ingratiate himself so thoroughly in an entirely foreign culture that when he finally returned to Venice in 1299 with a book detailing his adventures, he became the most famous explorer of the day.[96]

The facts and figures in the book, *The Travels of Marco Polo*, were so exotic and out of the norm for readers in Italy and Europe that despite its immense success, it was often considered a glorious fiction. Indeed, even some modern historians and researchers question the details of Polo's book, which was actually written by Rustichello da Pisa, but that first impression of the Far East remains an important part of the history of Western civilization. It was perhaps even one of the fundamental inspirations behind the growing interest in higher education—a crucial aspect of the Renaissance. Although Marco Polo's journeys and written renderings of the fascinating far side of the world sparked a yearning for knowledge and discovery in

---

[93] McNeese, Tim and William H. Goetzmann. *Marco Polo and the Realm of Kublai Khan.* 2009.

[94] "Marco Polo and his Travels." *Silk Road Foundation.* Web.

[95] Ibid.

[96] Ibid.

Venetians and other Europeans, Italy was hit hard by a fearsome bout of plague in the mid-14th century, curtailing any such expeditions.

The Black Death was so serious and widespread that it killed about a third of the population of Europe. The Republic of Florence and the Republic of Venice were among the worst of Europe's plague cities. In Florence, 60 percent of the population died within just a few months.[97] Agnolo di Tura, a historian from Siena, Italy, recorded his experiences with the sickness:

> All the citizens did little else except to carry dead bodies to be buried [...] At every church they dug deep pits down to the water-table; and thus those who were poor who died during the night were bundled up quickly and thrown into the pit. In the morning when a large number of bodies were found in the pit, they took some earth and shovelled it down on top of them; and later others were placed on top of them and then another layer of earth, just as one makes lasagne with layers of pasta and cheese.[98]

The medieval Italians persevered, and when the death toll finally started to decline, the Florentines and Venetians leaped wholeheartedly into the new day. They embraced art, architecture, literature, and science once more as their early Roman ancestors had done a millennium before. Some of the world's most influential polymaths, including Leonardo da Vinci and Michelangelo, perfectly encapsulated the lost Classical ideals of literature, art, philosophy, and science. They inspired the lasting term "Renaissance Man."[99] Thanks to the epic examples set by Marco Polo and his fellow Italians, Europe

---

[97] Ibid.

[98] Di Tura, Agnolo. Cited in William M. Bowsky's *The Black Death: A Turning Point in History?* 1971.

[99] Hall, M. C. *Leonardo da Vinci: The Famed Renaissance Man.* 2010.

as a whole moved into the Renaissance period about a century later, embracing art, literature, exploration, and philosophy anew.

Chapter 15 – Joan of Arc

Of the love or hatred God has for the English, I know nothing, but I do know that they will all be thrown out of France, except those who die there.

(Jeanne d'Arc, translated from trial records of March 15, 1431)

While the Republic of Venice blossomed with philosophy and art, Western Europe declared ceaseless war on itself. The English House of Plantagenet and the French House of Valois had been fighting over the right to rule France since 1337 in the Hundred Years' War, and they were still at it in the mid-15th century. English kings following in the dynastic footsteps of William the Conqueror claimed land rights in Normandy, Anjou, and other parts of the French realm, even though they had been politically separate from those regions since 1204.[100] The House of Valois, fully French and in possession of the majority of the disputed lands, would not yield to English demands.[101]

In the 500 years that had passed since France, Normandy, and England were made kin through conquest, the royal families of each region intermarried frequently and strategically enough that any of them could lay claim to virtually all of England and France. The result was constant warfare between the kingdoms and ever-changing borders

---

[100] Philip II of France conquered Normandy for France in 1204.

[101] Tout, T.F. *The History of England.* 1969.

delineating England and France. Until 1430, there was little hope in sight for the citizens and soldiers of either side since successive monarchs insisted on carrying out the desires of their predecessors.

The hero of the Hundred Years' War was a young girl called Jeanne d'Arc, better known as Joan of Arc.[102] Born in Domrémy, France, in 1412, she grew up in a poor farming family who didn't even own the land on which they grew their crops. Devoutly Catholic and mostly isolated during her youth, Joan of Arc was educated mostly by her mother. She was working alongside her family when, in 1422, a series of monarchal deaths left the thrones of both England and France to the infant King Henry VI of England.[103] The late and purportedly insane French king, Charles VI, had disinherited his own son, Charles VII, in favor of the English monarch.

Joan of Arc, after experiencing a series of religious visions, was compelled to speak with Charles VII, who still considered himself King of France. According to the girl, St. Michael, St. Catherine, and St. Margaret had visited her during a vision and insisted she contact Charles VII and ask his permission to lead the French army. Joan was convinced that she had been chosen by God to lead his people—that is, the Catholic French—to victory in battle. Once she had vanquished the English, she would reinstate Charles as the unquestioned ruler of all France.

Of course, contacting a king was not something that France's royal guard was prepared to let a poor farm girl do. She endeavored to see Charles anyway, following the voices and instructions in her visions to the village of Vaucouleurs some 300 kilometers (186 miles) east of Paris. There she waited several months, spanning between the years of 1428 and 1429, until her rising popularity with the villagers

---

[102] Bartolotta, K.L. *The Inquisition: The Quest for Absolute Religious Power.* 2017.

[103] "Henry VI." *Royal.uk.* Web.

impressed the leader of the local military garrison, Robert de Baudricourt.[104] Baudricourt gave the pious girl a horse and an escort to meet with Charles VII at his court.

After he was satisfied that Joan was at the very least a pure-hearted Catholic girl with his and France's best interests at heart, Charles equipped his strange visitor with armor and weaponry and sent her to the battlefield at Orléans. Confident, Joan told her patron that she would provide a sign from God when she reached the city. A few weeks after she joined the French troops there, the English were routed. According to the clergy present, the surrender of the English was the sign from God that Joan had promised.

The story of the girl with visions from God enraptured the people of France, from the poorest farmers and village traders to the most powerful members of the army and aristocracy. The royal family and the people of France had been faithful to the Catholic Church ever since the first days of the Holy Roman Empire and Charlemagne. Religious education was the most prominent type of studying any young people undertook, and their belief in the Christian doctrines was strong. Joan's story compelled the sympathy and pride of her entire nation and emboldened the French army to storm the English forces upon their lands and flush them out for good.

At the continued urging of Joan of Arc, Charles VII went to Reims to be crowned King of France in July of 1429. England, suffering its own internal succession between rival factions of the ruling House of Plantagenet, maintained that all of France was still in possession of the child King Henry VI. The English forces struggled to regain traction in France with so much infighting at home; however, their allies in the French region of Burgundy helped keep the war effort moving forward. When Joan of Arc was thrown from her horse in battle outside the city gates of Compiègne, the Burgundians took her

---

[104] Orgelfinger, G. *Joan of Arc in the English Imagination, 1429–1829.* 2019.

prisoner and sold her to the English in Normandy.[105]

England was considerably grateful for the chance to break the hallowed Maid of Orleans, as she was often called, and its lawmakers subjected her to several months of interrogation while she stayed in a military prison. The trial was soon handed over to the English clergy, who insisted Joan was a heretic. They told the 19-year-old soldier that it was against God's law for a female to dress like a man, to which she replied it was but a "little thing" in the eyes of the Lord. Furthermore, while imprisoned, Joan felt that it was necessary to wear thick leather pants as it protected her from the advances of ill-meaning guards. Nevertheless, it was the most damning piece of evidence to a tribunal of hyper-religious men who believed there were fundamental differences in the roles of men and women.

The trial was mostly politically motivated, as the English court wished to make a mockery of the so-called savior of France. Ultimately, Joan of Arc was found guilty of heresy by the English clergy and sentenced to death. [106] She was burned publicly at the stake on May 30, 1431, in Rouen, the capital city of Normandy.[107] She asked that the clergy hold crosses around her while the fire burned, and they complied, remaining there as she burned to death. When the fire burned out, the ashes were raked back and burned twice more to ensure no rumors of Joan's escape.

Even after her death, Joan of Arc's legendary story lived on in the hearts of the French people. She had managed to inspire whole armies of men to join the fight against England and reignite the hope of bringing the war to an end. The series of battles that followed the French victory at Orléans over the next 22 years were decisive indeed.

---

[105] Ibid.

[106] Barstow, A.L. *Joan of Arc: Heretic, Mystic, Shaman.* 1986.

[107] Ibid.

Charles VII's forces conquered Normandy and Aquitaine, leaving only Calais to the English by 1453.[108] Philip the Good of Burgundy switched sides and decided to support Charles VII as the true King of France, at which point the Hundred Years' War logistically came to an end. More battles would be fought, but England's rule over mainland Europe had all but ended.

The Catholic Church reinvestigated Joan of Arc's case from 1452 to 1456 and posthumously decided that she was not only innocent but a martyr of their cause.[109]

---

[108] Allmand, C. *The Hundred Years War: England and France at War C.1300-c.1450.* 1989.

[109] "Joan of Arc." *New World Encyclopedia.* Web.

Chapter 16 – Isabella I of Castile

I will assume the undertaking for my own crown of Castile, and am ready to pawn my jewels to defray the expenses of it, if the funds in the treasury should be found inadequate.

(Queen Isabella I)[110]

Spanish rulers saw how obedience to the Holy Roman Emperor and the Catholic Church had unified France and much of Central Europe, and they sought to make the same arrangement for themselves. At the beginning of the 15th century, the kingdoms of the Iberian Peninsula were only loosely connected, consisting of Aragon, Castile, and Portugal bordering the Atlantic Ocean. The Kingdom of Castile was the largest of these, stretching from the very top of the peninsula all the way south, almost touching the top of Africa. Portugal was relatively the same size as it is today, but the very south of modern Spain was inhabited by the Kingdom of Granada, and the eastern section contained the Kingdoms of Aragon, Navarre, and Catalonia. In the Mediterranean Sea lay the Kingdom of Majorca.

Heiress presumptive to the crown of Castile, Princess Isabella had a notoriously fierce and determined character that demanded respect from all she met, whether they were foreign dignitaries or servants. Her fundamental motivation in life was to prove her faith in the

---

[110] Isabella of Castile as quoted by William C. King in *Woman: Her Position, Influence, and Achievement*, 1903.

Catholic Church and lead the Christians of her realm to glory in the name of God. As a female, it was presumed that her first duty to her kingdom was to unite it with another through a political marriage. Her brother Henry IV, King of Castile, had agreed to make Isabella his heir if she would marry whom he chose for her. She had difficulty with this stipulation, however.

Having rejected the matrimonial proposal of Afonso V of Portugal in 1465 and praying for God to intervene in her betrothal to military general Pedro Girón Acuña Pacheco soon afterward, Isabella sought only a husband equal to her in faith and political ambition.[111,112] Miraculously, at least from Isabella's point of view, Pacheco died of a sudden sickness on his way to meet her. In 1469, the princess was happily married to her first choice of husband, Ferdinand II of Aragon.[113] Ferdinand was also the heir to the crown of his kingdom, which meant that their union connected the two largest and most powerful pieces of Spain.

When the devout Isabella inherited the crown of Castile from her brother in 1474, she shared it with Ferdinand without hesitation.[114] Alike in mindset and eager to formulate a plan for the future of Spain, the couple's first thoughts were of the religious purification of their people. Many subjects in Aragon and Castile were faithful to the Catholic Pope; however, they shared the land with others who practiced Jewish and Islamic religions. Before they could transform the religious landscape of Spain, the Catholic Monarchs—so-called by their peers—had to prove they could hold their thrones.

One year after Isabella and Ferdinand were given the crowns of

[111] Gerli, E.M. – Editor. *Medieval Iberia: An Encyclopedia.* 2003.

[112] Meyer, C. *Isabel: Jewel of Castilla.* 2000.

[113]Cowans, Jon (editor.) *Early Modern Spain: A Documentary History.* 2003.

[114]Kilsby, J. *Access to History: Spain 1469-1598 Second Edition.* 2015.

Castile, they became victims of a plot to replace the new queen with her niece, Joanna. King Afonso V of Portugal headed the would-be usurpation by marrying Joanna, the daughter of the late King Henry IV of Castile, to capitalize on his bride's claim to the crown of Castile. He then declared war and invaded Castile, only to fight an indecisive, year-long war that neither oppressed nor favored either side. At last, Ferdinand II outwitted his enemies by sending word to the capital cities of Spain and Europe that his own troops had beat the Portuguese at the Battle of Toro in March of 1476.[115] The celebrations of the apparent victors dampened the ongoing efforts of King Afonso who ultimately withdrew.

By that time, Isabella and Ferdinand had had a daughter, Isabella, Princess of Asturias. The queen hastily had her namesake officially named heir apparent of Castile, thereby solidifying her own hold on the throne. The war with Portugal was not over until three years later when Portuguese forces defeated those of Castile at sea near Guinea. Afterward, the Portuguese, still having failed to make any inroads into Castile on land, agreed to sign a treaty and put a stop to the fighting. Isabella insisted that she hold the throne of Castile but offered Afonso all the disputed lands in the North Atlantic, except the Canary Islands. She was forced to give up purported ownership of Portugal and accept that Joanna would remain there.

With the problem of succession and Portuguese invasion dealt with, Isabella and Ferdinand could turn to their pet project: ridding Spain of its non-Catholics. These were mostly members of Islam and people of the Jewish faith, both of which had been present in Spain for many centuries before the Kingdoms of Castile and Aragon had even existed.

Muslims had thrived in Spain for centuries, having emigrated from North Africa around 711 CE and overthrowing the reigning Visigoths

---

[115] Downey, K. *Isabella: The Warrior Queen*. 2014.

of the region.[116] For centuries, their presence on the Iberian Peninsula was combative. The Muslim Moors, as they were called, occupied the southern regions of Spain while Christian kingdoms occupied the north.[117] Through successive battles, the Moors were pushed farther and farther south until most of them occupied the Kingdom of Granada.

As for the Jewish population, they had lived within the Spanish kingdoms since the Roman age. The regime of the Moors allowed the Jewish people to practice their faith freely, and they prospered. The period of Spanish history after the Moors conquered the Catholic Visigoths is known as the Golden Age of Jewish culture in Spain. It was long over by the time Isabella and Ferdinand were crowned monarchs of Castile and Aragon, but great numbers of the Jewish faith still lived within fragmented Spain.

To eradicate non-Christians from their lands, the new power couple of Europe instated the Spanish Inquisition. Their appointed inquisitors were mobilized throughout the country and given legal recourse to obtain information however necessary. Officially, the purpose of the Inquisition was to imprison or execute non-Christians and seek out the Jewish and Muslim populace who had been baptized under Christian law. Isabella and Ferdinand believed that recent converts to Christianity were still practicing their own religious ceremonies and services in secret, and they wanted such behavior to be severely punished.

The Inquisition tore the two kingdoms apart, terrifying Christians and non-Christians alike. The inquisitors set their sights on anyone and everyone, trying determinedly to prove allegations of heresy. People found guilty of blasphemy or misconduct against the Catholic Church

---

[116] Hazbun, G. *Narratives of the Islamic Conquest from Medieval Spain.* 2015.

[117] Ibid.

were imprisoned, tortured, fined, or executed. Some of the thousands of victims of the Inquisition were publicly burned to death as a reminder to citizens how important it was to become and stay a good Christian.[118] Tens of thousands of people were questioned by inquisitors, and most of them were released after being found not guilty of crimes against the Church or the Crown. Of the king and queen, it was said that Ferdinand II was more prone to mercy while Isabella I was usually inclined toward sentencing. The queen cultivated a reputation as an iron-fisted ruler whose primary goals of purification outweighed her belief in compassion for the innocent.

While the terror of the Inquisition reigned within the borders of Aragon and Castile, Isabella turned her sights on the remainder of Spain. She felt that if her reign were to have the impact and deep meaning that she wanted, she would have to conquer and baptize all of Iberia. Her goal became achievable when, in 1479, Ferdinand became King of Aragon following the death of his father.[119] Fully in control of Aragon's military and financial resources, Ferdinand backed his wife fully as she declared war on the Kingdom of Granada less than three years later. The military campaign against the Moorish stronghold lasted ten years in total, though the battles were fought mostly during the springtime of those years. By January 2, 1492, Muhammad XII of Granada admitted defeat to his Catholic enemies and gave up his palace and the city of Granada.[120] All the Moors and Jewish within the annexed kingdom were forced to either convert to Christianity immediately or face deportation.

Of course, by 1492 Isabella had more to deal with than just the land within the confines of Europe.

---

[118] Murphy, C. *God's Jury: The Inquisition and the Making of the Modern World.* 2012.

[119] Faiella, G. *Spain: A Primary Source Cultural Guide.* 2004.

[120] Carr, M. *Blood and Faith: The Purging of Muslim Spain, 1492-1614.* 2010.

Chapter 17 – The Age of Discovery

I believe it was God's will that we should come back, so that men might know the things that are in the world, since...no other man, Christian or Saracen, Mongol or pagan, has explored so much of the world as Messer Marco, son of Messer Niccolo Polo, great and noble citizen of the city of Venice.

(Marco Polo, *Book of the Marvels of the World*)

The Renaissance brought with it a yearning for knowledge and a strong desire to see everything the world had to offer. Strong kingdoms with the resources to fund exploratory missions across land and sea took their chances as much in an attempt to curb the potential colonial spread of their neighbors as to make any genuine discoveries. As always, financial gain was more important than discovery for discovery's sake; so, it was with commercialism in mind that monarchs sent their most skilled naval officers on such expeditions.

Trade and international exploration were nothing new to the people of the Mediterranean, whose Greek counterparts had been mostly absorbed into the Turkish Ottoman Empire. The Holy Roman Empire was also an old hand at seafaring ventures, but its internal structure was far too fragmented to arrange for an international venture. The Republic of Venice had already cornered the market on Asian spices and was unprepared to break the status quo. The Netherlands and

Scandinavia were mostly distracted by their participation in religious wars, and that left most of the exploration in the hands of Western Europe.

The western nations of the continent had long been excluded from the excitement of overseas exploration due to their far position from the Mediterranean center of transit, but with updated shipping technologies in place, they were eager to make up for it. Outdated overland trade routes into Asia gave ship captains the excuse they were looking for to sail east. Asian spices, tea, and silks were immensely popular with aristocratic Europeans, and merchants stood to lose their livelihoods if the old routes could not be replaced.

Portugal, a traditionally strong seafaring nation, set out earlier than its peers. In the first part of the 15th century, Prince Henry the Navigator began sailing down the western length of Africa, founding Portuguese villages and expanding his existing maps.[121] Fernão Gomes picked up where Prince Henry had left off and further developed Portuguese trade with Africa, resulting in peppers, gold dust, and foreign slaves. The slave trade proved to be a huge financial boon for the impoverished Portuguese crown, but it still wanted to find a way to trade directly with India.

In search of India, Christopher Columbus, an Italian explorer, decided on a unique solution; he would sail west instead of east and reach India from its eastern coast. After years of petitioning, King Ferdinand and Queen Isabella of Castile decided to give Columbus the chance he so desired. In 1492, he set sail for India and 79 days later set foot on an island in the Bahamas.[122] At first believing the native people he saw there to be Indians, he called them "Indios." It's difficult to say when it became apparent that Columbus and his crew had found an

---

[121] Gallagher, A. *Prince Henry, the Navigator: Pioneer of Modern Exploration.* 2003.

[122] Murdock, J.B. *The Cruise of Columbus in the Bahamas, 1492.* Web.

altogether different people—members of the so-called New World.

The discovery of an entirely unknown continent was unprecedented. King John II of Portugal may have missed the chance to claim all the New World for himself, but he did not hesitate to send his own scouts after 1492 in order to capitalize on all the gold Columbus claimed to have found there. Other nations flocked west to see for themselves and to claim a piece of the treasures that lay there. Spain and Portugal were the first European nations to plant their flags in what came to be called the Americas.

Strategically, King John III (successor to Manuel I, who was heir to John II) still had India in his sights. He believed that he could reach India by sailing all the way around Africa, but without any correct maps, his theory could not be proven. A sailor called Vasco da Gama took up the challenge and successfully rounded Africa before touching ground in Calicut, India.[123] With the route secured, commercial trade with India began in earnest, and Portugal became the first European entity to establish its own trading center and factories there.

It was Spain, however, that profited the most during Europe's Age of Discovery. The brutal, violent regime at home was mirrored overseas in the Americas where Spanish conquistadors, such as Hernán Cortés, demolished the existing cultures and their leaders. Cortés led a major attack on the Aztec nation of modern Mexico City in 1521, claiming the city and its surrounding regions for Spain.[124] Vast numbers of the native peoples were murdered at Cortés' command as he took charge of the administration of the Spanish crown's "New Spain," which reached down into South America. He and his people stripped the cities of their considerable golden objects and sent them back to

---

[123] Koestler-Grack, R.A., Goetzmann, W.H. *Vasco Da Gama and the Sea Route to India.* 2006.

[124] Zronik, J.P. *Hernando Cortés: Spanish Invader of Mexico.* 2006.

Europe to fill the coffers of King Charles I of Spain (who was also Holy Roman Emperor Charles V).

England's involvement in the New World was minimal at first, as was that of France. Queen Elizabeth I of England was hard-pressed to send her most capable naval officers and ships to the Americas when she faced the constant threat of war from Spain. As Spain grew ever wealthier and more powerful on the international stage, however, the English and French had little choice but to try to divide what they could of the New World among themselves. Spain and Portugal had already claimed much of Mexico and Brazil, respectively, but there was still plenty of land in the northern continent that had yet to be stolen for Europe.

France, England, the Netherlands, Denmark, Sweden, Spain, and Portugal spent the bulk of the next century agreeing upon their borders within North and South America, while the people who already inhabited those continents were killed, subdued, or given promises of future compromise. Eventually, the entire landmass was claimed under European authority, and Portugal moved its capital city to Rio de Janeiro, Brazil.[125] People from Germany, Italy, Sweden, Denmark, the Netherlands, Scotland, and the tiny Duchy of Courland sailed west to build their own colonies as well, and these all had a hand in the shaping of the Americas in the modern age.

With the bulk of the world mapped and divided among the strongest states, Europe's wealth grew exponentially. So, too, did the need of its people to expand their knowledge of the ever-growing world they were a part of.

---

[125] Melvin Eugene Page, M.E. and Sonnenburg, P.M. *Colonialism: An International, Social, Cultural, and Political Encyclopedia, Volume 1.* 2003.

Chapter 18 – The Reformation

Alas, how can the poor souls live in Concord when you preachers sow amongst them in your sermons debate and discord? They look to you for light and you bring them darkness. Amend these crimes, I exhort you, and set forth God's word truly, both by true preaching and giving a good example, or else, I, whom God has appointed his vicar and high minister here, will see these divisions extinct, and these enormities corrected...

(King Henry VIII, *Fox's Book of Martyrs*)

The more reverence for education and philosophy, the more variance people discovered in their personal belief systems. Religious doctrine came under ideological scrutiny by the aristocracy whose loyalty the Catholic Church had relied upon for centuries. By the time the European powers were dividing up North and South America, the home front was already splintered into sections of Catholic strongholds and Protestant realms.

The aptly named Protestant religion is usually noted by historians to have begun in 1517 with the publishing of Martin Luther's pamphlet, the *Ninety-Five Theses*, also known as the *Disputation on the Power of Indulgences*.[126] Luther, a citizen of German lands within the Holy

---

[126] Marshall, Peter. *1517: Martin Luther and the Invention of the Reformation*. 2017.

Roman Empire, hoped to inspire a reorganization of the Catholic Church. Luther's main issue with Catholicism was the ability of wealthy individuals to buy what the church called "indulgences," which were payments in lieu of good deeds that were meant to counter one's sins.[127] Believing that this was a misuse of power, Luther wrote in favor of removing what he saw as a profitable business from religious life. Church officials refuted Luther's work vehemently, and the man found himself ostracized and excommunicated by the church in 1521.[128]

Despite these challenges, Martin Luther had indeed inspired change within many important people in Europe, particularly in parts of the Holy Roman Empire. The overwhelming desire of German states of the empire to become officially Protestant was potentially devastating to the Holy Roman Empire, ruled at the time by Charles V.[129] Grandson to the Catholic Monarchs themselves, Isabella and Ferdinand of Spain, Holy Roman Emperor Charles V was personally very dedicated to the cause of Catholicism for which his family had fought so hard. After the Duke of Prussia, the Duke of Hesse, and the Duke of Saxony (local rulers throughout the northern Holy Roman Empire) all converted to Protestantism, Charles V was called upon by Pope Clement VII to put a stop to the spread of anti-Catholicism in his realm.[130,131]

In 1530, Charles V arrived in Augsburg to meet with the dukes and

[127] Edwards Jr, Mark U. *Printing, Propaganda, and Martin Luther.* 2004.

[128] History.com editors. "The Reformation." A&E Television Networks. Last updated September 1, 2018.

[129] Randell, Keith and Russel Tarr. *Access to History: Luther and the German Reformation.* 2008.

[130] Michelet, Jules and Martin Luther. *The Life of Martin Luther Gathered from His Own Writings.* 1846.

[131] Robertson, William. *The History of the Reign of the Emperor Charles V.* 1809.

other reigning princes of the Holy Roman Empire to discuss important business, including the perceived threat to Catholicism.[132] A formal diet, or assembly, was convened that June at which the rulers of states within the Holy Roman Empire were made to explain their Lutheran reforms and practices to the emperor.[133] The Augsburg Confession set forth a formal foundation for the beliefs of Lutherans in the "21 Chief Articles of Faith." This was followed with seven "abuses corrected," a series of statements where the Lutheran faith was believed by its followers to have improved upon traditional Catholic doctrine.

As Martin Luther had suggested in the *Disputation on the Power of Indulgences*, the Lutheran articles of faith stated that a Christian could only be redeemed from sin by good deeds and not by payments to the church. The articles also allowed for Lutheran priests to marry, as well as for its followers to forego religious fasts and holidays.[134] In response, Charles V and Vatican advisors wrote a text refuting most of the Lutheran document, prompting another response from the Lutheran leaders in the form of the *Apology of the Augsburg Confession*. The *Apology* was a misnomer in that its authors intended no such thing. The *Apology* was first published in 1531, less than a year after the Diet of Augsburg. A second draft was soon penned, with input from Luther himself, and this was formally signed by the members of the newly formed Schmalkaldic League.[135] The League, comprised of Lutheran princes of the Holy Roman Empire, promised to band together in the event that any of them were attacked by Charles V.

---

[132] Lampart, Mark A. *Encyclopedia of Martin Luther and the Reformation.* 2017.

[133] A "diet" in this context refers to "the general deliberative assembly of the empire." Ibid.

[134] Ibid.

[135] Ibid.

In England, Protestantism was at the forefront of King Henry VIII's mind for one main reason: Divorce. His reasoning probably had very little to do with a change of faith; Tudor was raised Catholic, as was the norm in his realm, and by all accounts, he was a true believer in his religious teachings. The real reason he looked beyond the rules of the Catholic Church had everything to do with the fact that he wanted a separation from his wife, Catherine of Aragon, due to the fact that she was past child-bearing age. Henry Tudor was the ultimate patriarch in search of a legitimate son to rule England after he died. And he would settle for nothing less.

Protestants (a general term used to define Lutheranism and other similar reformed faiths) were allowed to divorce without papal consent. Though Martin Luther himself was not in favor of the English king divorcing his wife, Henry did eventually find a way to use the Reformation in his own favor. He appointed an ally, Thomas Cranmer, in the vacant position of Archbishop of Canterbury and had him judge in favor of a lawful royal divorce.[136] To reinforce the decision, Henry pronounced himself head of the Church of England, ending the Pope's authority there. The split from Catholic Europe was achieved, and that same year, King Henry wed his new bride, Anne Boleyn. Boleyn's family was very supportive of the English Reformation, not in small part because Anne's queenship depended on it.

Thus, it was almost entirely upon the whims of King Henry VIII that England changed from a stoic Catholic nation into a Protestant kingdom at the forefront of European religious reformation. The Church of England retained many likenesses to Roman Catholicism and ultimately answered to the oft-spontaneous decrees of King Henry VIII instead of the doctrines of Luther or any other Protestant philosopher of the day. When the *Apology of the Augsburg Confession*

---

[136] Wylie, James Aitken. *The History of Protestantism*. 1882.

was translated into English in 1536 and Henry was offered membership in the Schmalkaldic League, the king did not join.[137] That same year, he had his Protestant queen beheaded for treason and married his next wife, Jane Seymour, his third wife out of six.[138]

---

[137] Ibid.

[138] Ridgeway, Claire. *The Fall of Anne Boleyn: A Countdown.* 2015.

Chapter 19 – The Enlightenment

No man has received from nature the right to give orders to others. Freedom is a gift from heaven, and every individual of the same species has the right to enjoy it as soon as he is in enjoyment of his reason.

(Denis Diderot, *L'Encyclopédie*)

Armed with literacy, books, scientific tools, complex mathematics, and evolving political and religious ideologies, 18th-century Europe considered itself quite advanced indeed. The middle classes of the land had expanded to such a degree that more citizens than ever before were able to acquire a basic education and learn how their world was organized. More and more, it seemed, both the common people and much of the aristocracy could agree that reforms were necessary for the betterment of all. A principal philosophy of the time was the separation of church and state.[139]

For more than a thousand years, the poor and aristocratic alike had cowered under the immense shadow of the Catholic Church. Taught that to follow the church and the law of the monarchy was equivalent to saving one's soul, people's lives had been truly ruled by priests, bishops, cardinals, kings, queens, and popes. Though specific laws varied from kingdom to kingdom, it was usually mandatory for citizens to attend local church services and pay tithes to their

---

[139] Black, J. *Eighteenth Century Europe, 1700-89.* 1990.

ministers. In exchange, the various Christian-based churches of the day claimed to teach their congregations how to avoid going to hell and suffering for all eternity following their deaths. People were genuinely fearful of the wrath of God and the treachery of Satan, and they relied on the advice and instructions of the clergy to keep them safe.

The appearance of wider educational curriculums for the wealthy and middle classes during the 17th and 18th centuries provided different perspectives of humanity's role in the world. The sciences and economic philosophy gave people a glimpse into the natural world, administration, and means of production, and people began to foster serious doubt in organized religion. Emboldened by their ideas, people started to gather secretly and speak against the authority of the church. Their hushed conversations rang with facets of humanism, this time even more liberal in nature. Reason and logic were suggested as the foundations of human behavior and decision-making in place of the self-appointed leadership in churches and palaces.

People began to openly discuss the potential benefits of individual freedom and the details of a democratic monarchal system. In France, Jean-Jacques Rousseau expanded on an ancient idea he called the "social contract," first described by Plato in his book *Crito*. Plato's ubiquitous character, Socrates, explained social contract as the informal agreement between rulers and citizens of a civilization. It was an agreement in which citizens agree to follow the rules (pay taxes, provide labor, etc.) of a king or governor in exchange for protection and social benefits (defensive structures, army, food availability). Rousseau, in his book *The Social Contract*, argued that contemporary monarchies and their governments had failed to uphold their end of the bargain. He posited that: "MAN is born free; and everywhere he is in chains. One thinks himself the master of others, and still remains a greater slave than they."

Of course, this was no good for the authoritative dynasties of the continent. In centuries past, they had dealt with such talk swiftly and violently; now, with multitudes of people in agreement—among them, the wealthiest of the land—monarchs were forced to either destroy their own people or come up with a new solution. The compromise reached by some rulers was that of a constitutional monarchy.

England's Glorious Revolution of the 17th century ensured such a political system for itself. This came after a civil war just a few decades before during which King Charles I was beheaded in 1649 for refusing to allow his government a reasonable modicum of authority.[140] His son, Charles II, was invited to rule as his successor, and after his death, the crown went to his brother, James II. Both Kings Charles and James did little to relieve the tension between the Crown and Parliament, however; so, in 1688, William of Orange decided to intervene.[141]

William III, more commonly known as William of Orange, the military general of Holland, was invited by enemies of King James II to advance with his army. The invitation was extended for one main reason: William's wife, Mary Stuart, was the daughter of King James II and therefore a logical successor. William and Mary both approved the plan and seized London while allowing James II to flee to Scotland. Legally documented as the abdication of the throne on the part of King James II, the seizure gave English Parliament the chance to place both Mary and William on dual thrones. In exchange for their positions, William and Mary signed the English Bill of Rights in 1689, thereby leaving the taxation of the kingdom to Parliament. The powers of the English monarchy were greatly reduced from that point forward with authority placed more and more with the government.

England's political changes reverberated throughout the continent and

---

[140] Spencer, Charles. *Killers of the King*. 2015.

[141] Childs, J. *The Nine Years' War and the British Army, 1688-1697*. 1991.

fueled anti-monarchal debates. France, in particular, was greatly influenced by the revolution of its close neighbor, especially during the rule of the opulent King Louis XV not a century later. The French royal family, the House of Bourbon by ancestry, represented the absolute height of contemporary fashion and trend during the 18th century, and in doing so, they taxed their kingdom remarkably.[142] Given their traditional political educations, the Bourbons believed that it was their duty to present a perfect, lavish front to their citizens. This tactic may have worked for hundreds of years, but the days of such arrogance and waste were numbered.

---

[142] Cunningham, L.S., Reich, J.J., Fichner-Rathus, L. *Culture and Values: A Survey of the Humanities, Volume 2.* 2016.

Chapter 20 – The French Revolution

Little by little, the old world crumbled, and not once did the king imagine that some of the pieces might fall on him.

(Jennifer Donnelly, *Revolution*)

At the opulent Palace of Versailles in the year 1774, two young members of the aristocracy were crowned King and Queen of France following the death of the boy's grandfather, King Louis XV. The new King Louis XVI was 19 years of age; the new Queen Marie Antoinette was 18.[143] Louis had been bred to rule France, and Marie had been groomed to rule from her childhood home in Austria. Unfortunately, the lessons they'd both been given on governance, economy, and the monarchy were not enough to help them balance the budget of a country in over its head with debt.

The old King Louis had lived a life of luxury for his entire adult life, keeping mistresses and wives lavishly clothed, housed, furnished, and fed. The Palace of Versailles was the epitome of that lifestyle; it was clad outside and in with gold filigree, and it was built with the purest white marble, along with painted ceilings to rival those done by the

---

[143] Carlyle, Thomas. *The French Revolution: A History.* 1934.

hand of Michelangelo himself. For his grandson and heir, Louis XV wanted him to have the same kind of life. It was what was expected of the royal family of France, and therefore, each king was taught to exude authority, luxury, class, and taste. The same was expected of the Queen of France, who was responsible for cultivating herself as a beacon of feminine fashion for the aristocratic ladies of her court.

The young Queen Marie was bored by politics, but she knew how to appreciate the finer things in life. Ostracized at court for being foreign-born and then for failing to become pregnant by the king, Marie turned to fashion and excess for company. Her gowns were rich and heavy, the fabrics dyed and patterned exclusively for her by specialist tradesmen who visited the Palace of Versailles regularly. The queen made a lasting impression on France and the world for her elaborate wardrobe and towering hairstyles, but her husband earned fame for taking his heavily indebted nation to war in America.

King Louis XVI bowed to the pressure of his parliament in sending French troops over the Atlantic to support America in its bid for independence from Britain. Realistically, he wanted to send just enough support to win the loyalty of Americans while helping to financially exhaust Britain, against whom his own country had recently fought the Seven Years' War.[144] The war, which involved many European allies and enemies over the ownership of Silesia, was a means for Britain and France to gain the upper hand in North America and India—two areas where both kingdoms had large investments and colonies. King Louis XVI was convinced that keeping America and Britain at odds was the best thing for its own vested interests.

The expenditure, though relatively low, was still a huge strain on the already overburdened French economy. Historians believe that without the help of France, the United States of America would not

---

[144] "Seven Years' War." *Encyclopaedia Britannica*. Web.

have won its independence from the British monarchy, but there were few positive results for the monarchy of France.[145] The aristocracy, middle class, and working class were all restless, demanding an end to taxation and a solution to the bread shortage. The king had no way to pay his debts except to raise taxes on the French nobility, who flatly refused to participate in such reforms. While the king tried frantically to regain some authority over his people, the Third Estate appeared and made a move to gain some power for itself.

The Third Estate was a group of traditionally impotent and impoverished French citizens who were neither aristocratic nor members of the powerful Catholic clergy. Emmanuel Joseph Sieyès, inspired by the humanist and egalitarian philosophies of the Enlightenment, proposed that the disenfranchised citizens of France should band together and make their voices heard alongside the customary First and Second Estates—that is, the clergy and the nobles, respectively.[146]

Buoyed by the possibilities, the workers of France united and created the National Assembly, a parliamentary body completely outside the authority of the king and comprised of many members of the Jacobin Club. The Jacobins, also known as the Society of Friends of the Constitution, was an extreme political group that called for the removal of the monarchy altogether.[147] The Assembly was joined over the course of the next few months by a majority of clergy members and a small portion of the nobility. They committed themselves to write a French constitution, and in 1791, they accomplished that

---

[145] Louis XVI in the American Revolution." *Encyclopedia of the American Revolution: Library of Military History.* Web. 2006.

[146] Sieyes, Emmanuel Joseph. *Emmanuel Joseph Sieyes: The Essential Political Writings.* 2014.

[147] "Jacobin Club." *Encyclopaedia Britannica.* Web.

goal.[148] In September of that year, King Louis XVI signed the constitution, effectively recreating France as a constitutional monarchy.

King Louis had no choice but to relinquish his power since the mob in Paris had already kidnapped the royal family from the Palace of Versailles and moved them into the heart of the city during the riots in October of the previous year. The family made a failed escape attempt shortly before Louis was forced to sign the constitution and forfeit centuries of absolute monarchy in France. The very next year, the National Assembly, rebranded as the National Convention, announced that France was an independent republic. King Louis XVI was beheaded by the guillotine in 1793 followed by Queen Marie Antoinette a few months later.[149] Their children were imprisoned.

What followed would come to be known as the Terror: a ten-month period of violence and assassinations under the leadership of the influential Jacobin Maximilien Robespierre. Ostensibly fighting counterrevolutionaries and foreign armies whose own monarchs had declared war on the new republic of France, Robespierre and his regime orchestrated the deaths of up to 40,000 people before falling victim to the guillotine himself.[150] When the internal turmoil died down, France reorganized itself politically and created the Directory, a five-member committee which ruled until 1799.[151] In that year, a popular military hero called Napoleon Bonaparte instigated a successful coup that made him the de facto leader of the nation.[152]

---

[148] Fitzsimmons, Michael P. *The Remaking of France: The National Assembly and the Constitution of 1791.*

[149] "The French Revolution." *PBS.* Web.

[150] Moes, Garry J. *Streams of Civilization.* 2003.

[151] "Directory French History." *Encyclopaedia Britannica.* Web.

[152] "Coup of 18-19 Brumaire French History." *Encyclopaedia Britannica.* Web.

Bonaparte had been the general of the French army before he became the nation's leader, and he was inclined to continue on in a similar vein during his dictatorship. The next 23 years were characterized by a series of battles and military conflicts known as the Napoleonic Wars.[153] War was first officially declared by Great Britain and its allies with the assassination of King Louis XVI. Though Holland and Spain were officially part of the war effort against France, Napoleon knew that his main enemy was Britain, whose navy had caused him great losses while on campaign in Egypt. Furthermore, there was continued strain between the two nations in vying for economic superiority within Europe and the matter of Britain's continued claim on French land.

Since the rule of England's King Edward III in the 14th century, England and then Britain had claimed ownership of some small part of France—be it Calais, Aquitaine, or Caen.[154] Once Napoleon seized power, Britain's King George III finally dropped the addendum to his title, "King of France," and officially recognized France as a republic.[155] King George III was not satisfied, however. He had lost America and France all in the space of 25 years, and he was wholeheartedly intent on British victory over Napoleon's forces. The English king declared war on France in 1803, only a year after the two countries had agreed upon peace.[156]

In 1804, Napoleon Bonaparte declared himself Emperor of France.[157] The next year, after successful attacks in Italy, he had himself crowned

[153] "Napoleonic Wars European History." *Encyclopedia Britannica*. Web.

[154] Corrigan, Gordan. *A Great and Glorious Adventure*. 2014.

[155] Corrigan, Gordan. *A Great and Glorious Adventure*. 2014.

[156] "Timeline: Napoleonic Wars." *Oxford Reference*. Web.

[157] Dwyer, P. *Citizen Emperor: Napoleon in Power*. 2013.

King of Italy in Milan before pushing farther into Austria.[158] After defeating the allied forces of Austria, Prussia, and Russia, Napoleon convinced Tsar Alexander I of Russia to enter into a political treaty with France in which they would join forces and divide Europe between themselves.[159] The tsar agreed in 1807, and together, the two emperors attacked Spain and Portugal, causing the Portuguese royal family to flee to Brazil for safety.[160]

By 1812, Napoleon had control of France, Spain, Portugal, Italy, Naples, the Confederation of the Rhine, and the Illyrian Provinces.[161] Greedily, the emperor decided to forego his treaty with Tsar Alexander I and went so far as to attack his ally with 600,000 soldiers on Russian soil.[162] Russia pulled away, defeated, but Moscow was ordered to be evacuated and burned before Napoleon pursued the tsar's soldiers there. When the flames died down, Napoleon occupied the Kremlin and waited for his ex-ally to concede defeat; instead, the Russian army descended upon the French and forced them to retreat. By the time the French made it back to Paris, Napoleon had lost half a million troops to the Russians.[163]

All of Western Europe was still at the mercy of the great French general, but Great Britain remained independent. The British navy held fast, decisively keeping enemy forces away from its shores, and waged war for its life. Prussia changed sides to join Great Britain and Russia in 1814, and the allied forces began to gain some traction

---

[158] "Timeline: Napoleonic Wars." *Oxford Reference*. Web.

[159] Nicolls, David. *Napoleon: A Biographical Companion*. 1999.

[160] Timeline: Napoleonic Wars." *Oxford Reference*. Web.

[161] *Carte de l'Empire Francais 1812*: Dresse par A.H. Dufour.

[162] "Alexander I Emperor of Russia." *Encyclopedia Britannica*. Web.

[163] Timeline: Napoleonic Wars." *Oxford Reference*. Web.

against the onslaught of the French Empire.[164] Paris was captured by the allies that same year, and Napoleon abdicated his throne before being sent to the island of Elba in exile.

Rallying, with the support of a military regiment and a small fleet of ships, Napoleon boldly slipped away from Elba the very next year to reclaim his empire. Quickly caught up in a battle with English and Prussian forces, the emperor was finally defeated at the Battle of Waterloo, then part of the United Kingdom of the Netherlands, on June 18, 1815.[165] Exiled once more on the island of St. Helena, Napoleon remained there until his death in 1821.[166] The Napoleonic Era was followed by a Bourbon Restoration in which the brothers of murdered King Louis XVI ruled in succession.[167] The Restoration kings reigned over a very moderated constitutional monarchy until Charles X attempted to rule with all the authority of his ancestors and was forced to abdicate. There were no more royal restorations after that point, as most of France was quite determined to govern itself.

---

[164] Ibid.

[165] Ibid.

[166] Hindmarsh, J. Thomas. *The Death of Napoleon: The Last Campaign.* 2007.

[167] Carpenter, K. *Refugees of the French Revolution.* 1999.

Chapter 21 – The Industrial Age

The history of the industrial revolution shows how that power passed from the king and the aristocracy to the bourgeoisie. Universal suffrage and universal schooling reinforced this tendency, and at last even the bourgeoisie stood in fear of the common people. For the masses promised to become king.

(Edward L. Bernays, *Propaganda*)

Science had come full force into European life by the 18th century. Building upon the mathematical and physical principles established by their predecessors, Europe's best minds were able to create powerful machines intended to increase the labor capacity of its workers. These machines not only made it possible for craftspeople and tradespeople to produce fabrics, foods, and tools more quickly than ever, but they also changed the entire way Europe's labor force worked.

Until that point, the working people of the continent had used virtually the same techniques as their ancestors, going back generations. Farmworkers plowed with iron tools dragged by horses and oxen then sowed seeds and waited for their crops to grow. In the meantime, they cared for vegetable gardens and livestock, including dairy animals. In the summer and autumn, farmers worked long hours cutting and hauling hay and grain and processing the cereals they harvested from the fields. Winter was a long and well-earned rest before the work started again in the spring.

While men mostly spent their time in the field or working with metals, women did most of the textile work that kept Europe clothed and warm. Traditional wool had been eclipsed by the use of cotton, which was mostly imported from the United States of America. These imports were briefly stalled in the late 18th century during the American Revolution, in which the United States fought against Britain to shake off the imperial rule of the crown, but it picked up again quickly as both sides depended heavily on the cotton trade. Once the United States won the war, it was necessary to continue cotton sales to help recoup the expenses of the military campaign.

With the advent of machines like Eli Whitney's cotton gin, workers were able to turn out swathes of clean cotton much more quickly. His invention, patented in the United States in 1794, mechanically separated cotton fibers from their seeds, a process that was painstaking and tedious when done by hand.[168] The cleaned cotton fibers were then brushed and spun into threads, which were either sold in spools or used to weave bolts of fabric. These bolts and spools were exported to Europe, along with raw, unprocessed cotton. The latter was considerably cheaper; therefore, it was the choice of many budget-conscious European manufacturers.

Unprocessed cotton or wool was brought to factories mostly in Great Britain, Germany, and Spain, where large textile plants had been constructed. Thanks to the 1764 invention of James Hargreaves of England, spinning no longer depended on slow tools like drop-spindles as it had in the Middle Ages. Hargreaves' spinning jenny allowed Europe's mostly female textile workers to create eight threads at once, instead of one.[169] As the invention was fine-tuned, those initial eight threads increased to as many as 120. The spinning jenny

---

[168] Lakwete, A. *Inventing the Cotton Gin: Machine and Myth in Antebellum America.* 2003.

[169] Gehani, R. *Management of Technology and Operations.* 1998.

and cotton gin, combined with John Kay's 1733 flying shuttle, completely revolutionized the textile manufacturing process from a cottage industry into a huge manufacturing endeavor.[170]

Though textiles were the main objective of these early industrial capitalists, each of their large-scale businesses was founded on another major invention: the steam engine. Before universal electrical networks, heavy machinery was powered by engines based on a design by Thomas Savery. Savery's invention, the Miner's Friend, was built in 1698 to pump water out of a coal mine using the power of superheated steam. The original device was only useful to a certain depth, but the revamped model—invented by Thomas Newcomen and his assistant John Calley in 1712—included a piston to control the movements of a mechanical pump.[171] The improved steam engine was soon used to power everything from the cotton gin to the power loom.

To heat the water and create enough steam to keep a factory full of machines running all day, industrialists needed a lot of coal. Because of the endless need for coal, the mining industry boomed alongside the factory textile industry, and in the space of just a few decades, England was transformed. Sheffield and York were consumed by factories, smokestacks, black smoke, and soot. The pollution pouring out from the spinning, weaving, and sewing factories stuck to homes and public buildings, thickening the air and devastating the air quality of the cities. With citizens choking whenever they went outside, laws were put in place that required factories to build their chimneys higher and higher, dumping the smoke into the clouds to theoretically disperse.

Independent workers and craftspeople were quickly outpaced by the unprecedented output of factory spinners, weavers, and clothmakers.

---

[170] Berman, B. *From Assets to Profits: Competing for IP Value and Return*. 2008.

[171] Lamb, Robert. "How Steam Technology Works." *HowStuffWorks*. Web.

Factory owners packed machines and operators into commercial spaces by the dozens and then by the hundreds, trying to turn bigger and bigger profits. The early days in the Industrial Revolution were disorderly and dangerous, characterized by machine malfunctions, serious accidents, and poorly paid employees. Industry on such a massive scale had never been attempted before, and there were as many problems as there were benefits. Workers struggled with long hours, no health care, and very little training on the machines.

In Great Britain, where the industrial cities of Sheffield and York led the way for the rest of the continent in terms of industry and commercialism, it was a time of incredible growth in terms of cityscapes, population, and even the concept of equality and women's rights. From one perspective, the Industrial Revolution gave the women of Europe the chance to earn a living for themselves and practice independence out in the city. On the other hand, both women and men were massively undervalued by their employers. Workers began to unionize and make demands of their employers to keep them safe and reasonably paid, and by 1833, Britain's Factory Act was passed by Parliament.[172]

The Factory Act improved conditions somewhat for early 19th-century laborers, but its standards were shockingly low in comparison with modern industry. One of its tenets, for example, was the rule that no children under the age of nine years could be employed. Of the remaining children—and there were thousands—those under the age of 13 were allowed to work up to 9 hours a day. Children 13 to 18 could work up to 12 hours per day. Conditions were often horrible for adults and children working in these factories, with few breaks and hot, uncomfortable working environments.

Following the Factory Act, inspectors were meant to be on site at every factory to ensure the rules were followed; unfortunately, not

---

[172] Kirby, P. *Child Workers and Industrial Health in Britain, 1780-1850.* 2013.

even this rule was strictly enforced. The following is a testimony of one such inspector upon visiting a factory without an appointment:

> My Lord, in the case of Taylor, Ibbotson & Co., I took the evidence from the mouths of the boys themselves. They stated to me that they commenced working on Friday morning, the 27th of May last, at six A.M., and that, with the exception of meal hours and one hour at midnight extra, they did not cease working till four o'clock on Saturday evening, having been two days and a night thus engaged. Believing the case scarcely possible, I asked every boy the same questions, and from each received the same answers.[173]

Conditions were rarely better in Germany and Spain, where textiles, glassware, and ironworks were being produced in factories. Germany was rich in iron ore and coal deposits, making it an ideal center of industry. The Napoleonic Wars contributed to the lag German industrialists experienced next to their British counterparts, but in the mid-19th century, it was already surpassing Great Britain in terms of output. In the Friedrich Wilhelm Ironworks near Mulheim in Germany, workers used the most modern British methods to streamline the production of high-quality iron. They burned a distilled form of coal, called coke, to more effectively smelt iron from iron ore. Not only did this innovation create pure, high-grade iron, but the emissions produced by burning coke were much cleaner than coal.

Coke-fueled smelting ovens were constructed to keep the iron separate from the fire's fuel, unlike Iron Age forgers who believed coal made the end product stronger. Keeping the iron free of additives turned out to be a much better method. Friedrich Harkort and Hermann Dietrich Piepenstock also created the puddling process to produce their iron, which increased output even more. Puddling was usually done by simply stirring the molten metal to expose it to

---

[173] "1822 Factory Act." *The National Archives*. Web.

oxygen, thereby burning off the excess carbon. These and other smelting innovations resulted in a purity so fine it needed a new name: steel.

The steel form of iron was much stronger than other iron alloys, which made it perfect for industrial-scale building. Ships, skyscrapers, bridges, factories, warehouses, stoves, and furnaces were constructed with the new material, physically changing the European urban landscape even further. Buildings were bigger and stronger, which inspired architects and designers to ever greater heights. While the first part of the Industrial Revolution used mass-produced fine iron purely for infrastructure, the latter part introduced the material in new, more artistic ways.

1779 saw the construction of the aptly named Iron Bridge at Shropshire, England.[174] A century later, in 1889, Gustave Eiffel's iron tower was constructed in central Paris as a kind of memento of the age. It marked the new era of industry and capitalism.[175]

---

[174] Langmead, D. and Garnaut, C. *Encyclopedia of Architectural and Engineering Feats*. 2001.

[175] Blanc, A., McEvoy, M., Plank, R. – Editors *Architecture and Construction in Steel*. 1993.

Chapter 22 – The British Empire of Queen Victoria

One general law, leading to the advancement of all organic beings, namely, multiply, vary, let the strongest live and the weakest die.

(Charles Darwin, *On the Origin of Species*)

The supreme and absolute power of the Church may have been gone by the time Queen Victoria ruled Great Britain, but religious faith and belief were far from it. Europe remained mostly divided between forms of Protestantism and Roman Catholicism, both of which had been officially separated from the inner workings of governments and monarchies. Britain, under Queen Victoria, prided itself on having cultivated an ideal balance between the love of God and the pursuit of science. In addition, it was the era of the British Empire, during which Great Britain became a colonial power as great as Spain had been during the Age of Discovery. Queen Victoria—and more importantly, her government—ruled over England, Scotland, Ireland, Wales, Canada, Australia, India, New Zealand, and parts of Africa.

Great Britain was the wealthiest and most industrialized nation in Europe. It was also taking steps to establish a better form of democratic election concerning the monarchy's government. The Great Reform Act of 1832 reorganized the divisions of England and

Wales so that their representatives could no longer be elected by means of the largest landowners, making an extra 250,000 men eligible to vote.[176] Scotland and Ireland followed suit in the same manner, greatly improving the influence the middle and lower classes had on government and policies.

Perhaps one of the most impressive changes in Britain during that era was the population increase, which exploded during the years of Victoria's reign, which lasted from 1837 to 1901.[177] There were about 13.9 million people in the kingdom when Queen Victoria first took the throne and as many as 32.5 million in the year she died. There are multiple posited reasons for this increase, including better science and health care, improving wages, and a trend toward large families. Also, the birth rate improved while the mortality rate declined, and most of this was thanks in some way to scientific endeavors.

Science battled on against religion in an endless war for supremacy, but science could not be stopped, even by the flocks of moralists that lived in Victorian Britain. Discoveries by Charles Darwin, an English naturalist by profession, shocked and horrified a great deal of people before they were accepted by mainstream science. It was his manuscript in particular, *On the Origin of Species*, that caused outrage by Christians against the new idea of biological evolution. In those pages, Darwin carefully outlined his research on various species of birds and mammals in the Galapagos Islands.

Darwin, educated in medicine at the University of Edinburgh, had become interested in the work of the French biologist Jean-Baptiste Lamarck while at school. Lamarck's studies in botany and zoology during the previous century had cemented Darwin's belief that the characteristics of one plant or animal could be inherited by its

---

[176] Evans, E. *The Great Reform Act of 1832*. 1983.

[177] Crouzet, F. *The Victorian Economy*. 1982.

seedlings or offspring. It was a fascinating study that could be used to help explain how certain varieties of food crops had come to change slowly over time from their original forms. For Charles Darwin, it explained even more about the natural world.

Darwin's journey to the Galapagos Islands introduced him to dozens of species he had either never seen before in person or which he had never even heard of. The geographical isolation of the islands provided the perfect environment in which those animals, birds, and insects—all presumably introduced to the island as exotic species—could find new means to meet their basic needs. Over time, they changed slightly to adapt to their new home but retained the overall appearance of their ancestors. Darwin noticed a variety of birds, for example, whose beaks had changed to better extract nourishment from exotic food sources. Examples were explained in plain terms in his book so the average reader could understand. Animals changed to adapt to their changing environments, Darwin argued, and the motivating factor behind those changes was natural selection.

Natural selection was a theory all Darwin's own. It stated that every animal and plant species on Earth was the product of the world around it. As explained in *On the Origin of Species*, natural selection is the process in which specific physical traits are preserved when they are advantageous genetic mutations. It was the same premise by which dogs had been bred for thousands of years in Britain: those dogs with the traits that breeders wanted to copy were bred together. Dogs with disadvantageous traits were kept out of the breeding pool.

Darwin's research and theories posited that animals and humans probably had a common ancestor—and church-going Victorians were not impressed at all. God created humans in his own image, they explained, and no one was related to apes. On the other end of the social spectrum, scientists pored over their editions of Darwin's book greedily, entranced by its implications in their own fields of research. The controversy and infighting between British subjects and the book's wider European and international audiences were extreme.

The Victorians, however, did pride themselves very highly on maintaining order and diplomacy, and unlike the days of the Reformation, blaspheming against the Church was no longer means for execution in Great Britain. Indeed, despite the social ostracization Darwin suffered from many groups following the publishing of his book, he was honored by his country with a burial at Westminster Abbey. His body was put to rest near that of Isaac Newton.

Thanks to the perseverance of scientists like Darwin, medicine evolved in leaps and bounds over the course of the 19th century. Physicians used autopsies more regularly to learn about death, as well as about the parts of the body and how they interacted with each other. Given the rise of the indomitable industrial era, respiratory issues were one of the most common causes of complaint and death. Cholera was also very high on the list, especially because many doctors and scientists had yet to fully embrace germ theory. When it did catch on, Louis Pasteur used its principles to create a vaccine for anthrax and rabies. Pasteur's work also led to new, safer methods for processing milk and dairy products, named pasteurization in his honor.

Chapter 23 – The Great War

Industrial Europe had enjoyed a mostly peaceful period of economic growth, scientific discovery, and spiritual evolution, but it did not last. Political structures were changing throughout the continent; the Ottoman Empire shrank away from Greece and the Eastern Mediterranean, and the Prussian Empire experienced devolutionary forces from within. Following a disastrous visit by Archduke Ferdinand of Austria-Hungary to its capital city of Sarajevo in 1914, allied nations quickly took up arms against one another.[178]

The violence was set off by Yugoslav nationalist Gavrilo Princip, a Serbian national in Bosnia, which was under the occupation of Austria-Hungary. Princip was a member of Young Bosnia with contacts in the Black Hand society. Young Bosnians were mostly teen and young adult students opposed to Austro-Hungarian authority over the Slavic people of the realm who had been under the administration of the empire since the late 19th century. The group actively campaigned for the empire to release the Slavs and Serbs from within their political grasp and allow the two cultures to establish their own nations.

Archduke Ferdinand was the heir presumptive to the Austria-

---

[178] Dedijer, Vladimir. *World War, 1914-1918.* 1966.

Hungarian crown in 1914, which was comprised of an emperorship of Austria and kingship of Hungary. Operating as the Dual Monarchy since 1867, the two realms were under the control of Franz Joseph I.[179] The presumptive succession of his realms lay on the shoulders of his nephew, Franz Ferdinand, after following the suicide of his only son Rudolph in 1889.[180] Ferdinand was publicly supportive of administrative reforms that would give the ethnic minorities of his realm more independence within the state. These political beliefs, diplomatic as they were, would prove to be his downfall. With social unrest mounting in Serbia and among Serbs within Austria-Hungary, it was no longer the will of all the people that a peaceful solution be found. The Black Hand, a secret Serbian society that employed violence to obtain freedom for Serbs, made the fateful decision that would throw Europe into one of the worst wars in its history.

The Black Hand, centered across the border in Serbia, supported the nationalist ideals of Gavrilo Princip and the Young Bosnians, as well as any other anti-Austro-Hungarian movements within their powerful neighbor. The unofficial leader of the Black Hand, Colonel Dragutin Dimitrijević, decided that the only way to ensure a revolution was to kill Archduke Ferdinand. Since Ferdinand was attempting to appease the Serbs diplomatically, Dimitrijević worried that his countrymen would be pacified and coaxed into accepting monarchal reforms instead of demanding their freedom; with the Archduke out of the way, a revolt would be much more likely. The Black Hand equipped Gavrilo and others with weapons and instructed them to kill the heir presumptive of the empire during his state visit to Sarajevo.[181]

The Archduke traveled to Sarajevo that fateful day in June of 1914 in

---

[179] Tschuppik, K. *The Reign of the Emperor Francis Joseph, 1848-1916.* 2017.

[180] Ibid.

[181] Combs, C. *Terrorism in the Twenty-First Century.* 2013.

order to inspect the military ranks stationed there. He arrived in the capital with his wife, Duchess Sophie Chotek. They were attacked with a hand grenade while touring in an open-top car on the morning of June 28th. The attempted assassination failed, injuring members of another car driving behind that of the Archduke and the Duchess. Undercover assassins spread out to cover various parts of the city, and the couple later reentered the open-top car to visit the victims of the attack at the local hospital. Serendipitously, traffic slowed the car down in the same spot where Gavrilo Princip was waiting.[182] He walked across the street, brandished his gun, and shot both Ferdinand and Sophie before fleeing the scene. The victims died shortly afterward.[183]

The ensuing political upheaval proved too great for mere diplomatic meetings between Serbia and Austria-Hungary. One month after the assassination, on July 28th, the Austria-Hungary declared war on Serbia.[184] Germany gave its full support to the Austro-Hungarian Empire; Russia gave its own to Serbia. That very night, Austria-Hungary began firing on the Serbian capital city of Belgrade.

Ironically, the German leader, Kaiser Wilhelm II, favored diplomatic discussions in place of war. His military generals disagreed, however, and having felt his authority waver in recent years, Wilhelm was compelled to go along with the war effort. His nation joined the Triple Alliance: Austria-Hungary, Germany, and Italy in opposition of the Triple Entente of Great Britain, France, and the Russian Empire.

---

[182] Many sources would have us believe that Gavrilo was not strategically planted at that spot but randomly eating a sandwich at the café in that location. Research by *Smithsonian* writer Mike Dash refutes the sandwich story. Read more in his *Smithsonian* article, "The Origin of the Tale that Gavrilo Princip Was Eating a Sandwich When He Assassinated Franz Ferdinand."

[183] Beyer, Rick. *The Greatest Stories Never Told.* 2003.

[184] Sharp, Alan. *28 June.* 2014.

These six nations were the central combatants of the First World War, even though the original feud had only been between Serbia and Austria-Hungary. Within the year, more than a dozen nations had officially sided with the Triple Entente against Kaiser Wilhelm II, including the United States, China, and Japan.

Fighting was fully under way by August, with Austro-Hungarians marching into Serbia, German soldiers in Luxemburg, and French and German armies facing off in the Duchy of Lorraine. Emperor Taishō of Japan put his own military resources on the line after forming an agreement with Great Britain that stated Japan could take Germany's holdings in the Pacific Ocean. The Ottoman Empire, under the subjugate leadership of Ismail Enver Pasha—representing Emperor Mehmed V—officially sided with Germany. Land claims and alliances on either side of the war effort were countless, as countries from every inhabited continent put a stake in the outcome of the massive power struggle.

Most of the battles took place in Western Europe, and during the first month, victories were numerous for Germany and Austria-Hungary. Later in the year, Britain provided relief troops via Canada and New Zealand which immensely helped to keep German forces from capturing Paris. Germany established itself as the major warmongering nation among all those within the Allies and the Axis. In 1915, the German army launched a chlorine attack on enemy troops, marking the beginning of the age of chemical warfare.[185] It was a tactic that the Allied forces quickly adopted for themselves, and after four years of fighting, nearly 1 million people had been killed or wounded from the use of chemical weapons.[186]

Almost immediately after the war began, Serbia was invaded by

---

[185] Ray, Michael. "Timeline of World War I." *Encyclopaedia Britannica*. Web.

[186] Ibid.

Austria-Hungary, Germany, and Bulgaria. Its own national troops were evacuated to Greece before rejoining the fight the following year when Montenegro fell victim to Austria-Hungary as well. Nearly all of 1916 was spent in violent bloodshed in the ongoing Battle of Verdun in France, while Britain and Germany faced off in the seas off the coast of Denmark.[187] It was the first all-out use of modern warfare and equipment, and France suffered the most damage of any nation under the treads and guns of tanks, cannon fire, and chlorine and mustard gas blasts. President Woodrow Wilson of the United States of America, having refrained from joining the feud, officially declared war on Germany in April of 1917 and headed arbitration discussions between the Allies and the Axis.[188]

By 1918, Wilson was able to convince Germany to accept an armistice, much to the chagrin of German troops who believed they had been winning the war.[189] Diplomacy was shaky, but it held for the time being, particularly because the Russian Empire had pulled out months prior to the ceasefire agreement on November 11, 1918.[190] At that point, Tsar Nicolas II had more pressing matters to attend to on the home front.

---

[187] Ibid.

[188] Ibid.

[189] Barth, Boris. "Stab-in-the-back Myth." *1914-1918 Online.* Web.

[190] Ray, Michael. "Timeline of World War I." *Encyclopaedia Britannica.* Web.

Chapter 24 – The Russian Revolution

Thus the Russian working class had contradictory characteristics for a Marxist diagnosing its revolutionary potential. Yet the empirical evidence of the period from the 1890s to 1914 suggests that in fact Russia's working class, despite its close links with the peasantry, was exceptionally militant and revolutionary.

(Sheila Fitzpatrick, *The Russian Revolution 1917-1932*)

Political revolution had been on the minds of all impoverished Europeans since the Middle Ages, and that was no less true in the far eastern reaches of the continent. Moscow and St. Petersburg, the most heavily populated cities of the Russian Empire, were west of the dividing Caucasus Mountains and largely involved in the affairs of Eastern European nations. In 1917, the Russian Empire was ruled by Tsar Nicolas II, and it included modern Poland, Finland, Lithuania, Latvia, Estonia, and part of Romania.[191] Rocked by the heavy burden of the Great War, the dynastic tsar's reign would soon come to an abrupt end that would send shockwaves throughout the whole world.

Over 50 years had passed since the royal family had abolished serfdom, an economic system not unlike that of Norman Britain, in which workers were given the right to live on the land of the tsar in

---

[191] Service, R. The Last of the Tsars: Nicholas II and the Russian Revolution. 2017.

exchange for providing the state with a portion of each harvest. All people had the right to own their own land, but little had changed for Russia's poorest people, who could still not afford to buy their own property. They remained stuck in rental agreements and prices set by landlords who could decide to evict whole families at any time. The ideals of the *Communist Manifesto*, a political pamphlet authored by Friedrich Engels, a German journalist, and Russian journalist Karl Marx had not been reached as had been previously hoped.

For a vast empire that had been oppressed by royal dynasties for more than three centuries, the glimmer of communism held hope for the poorest of Russia's people. Marx and Engels had formulated a political thesis based on communal sharing of all the products of the land within each nation, and in that system, all people were equal. Communism had no space for royalty, aristocracy, or oppressive managerial regimes; it posited that the means of production— agricultural land, tools, factories, and the like—should be in the hands of the laborers.

Still suffering at the turn of the 20th century, Russia's farmers and workers demanded change. The laborers in the cities had gone on strike in 1905,[192] causing massive worker shortages that stopped the empire's manufacturing sector in its tracks. Tsar Nicolas II, trying to appease his nation's most crucial workers, promised to create a people's government in which everyone could vote on their representatives. Nicolas II was already in a very precarious situation when he agreed to enter WWI beside Great Britain, France, and Serbia to defend against Austrian retaliation for Archduke Ferdinand's death.

The war heavily taxed an already agitated Russian populace who felt that being sent to war was the very final reason in a long list of reasons to rebel. In the last year of WWI, Russians crowded into the streets of St. Petersburg and cried out for bread. Striking industry workers

---

[192] Surh, G. *1905 In St. Petersburg: Labor, Society, and Revolution.* 1989.

joined them, demanding wage increases to cover their own costs of living. Imperial guards shot and killed some of the demonstrators but eventually cowed under the sheer volume of citizens. The tsar knew his time was done; he abdicated the throne in March of 1917, days after a group of wealthy citizens formed their own provisional government.[193] Abdication was not good enough for the most extreme revolutionaries, however, who held the royal family captive and eventually murdered them all.

For political party leader Vladimir Lenin and his followers, however, governance by the country's bourgeoisie was little better than dictatorship by the tsar. He rallied thousands of Russian soldiers, workers, and poor to descend upon the provisional government in November of the same year and call for its dissolution. The move was successful. Without so much as a single life lost, Lenin's Bolsheviks were empowered to organize the former Russian Empire into a brand-new communist nation. Vladimir Lenin himself was the leader of the people's government, but he refused to take any imperialist title to place himself above any other member of the government or citizenry.

Lenin pulled Russian troops out of the war, but they came home only to find Russia in a state of civil war. The Red Army, forged from Lenin's newly established Russian Communist Party, faced off against a mixed coalition of monarchists, democratic reformists, and bourgeoise capitalists. The measures Lenin took to empower his Red Army had a massively negative effect on the country's economy as a whole, and while the soldiers were fed, tens of thousands of other people starved.

Facing constant threats from his opposition and even an assassination attempt in 1919, Lenin established a secret police force called the

---

[193] Figes, Orlando. "From Tsar to U.S.S.R." *National Geographic History Magazine.* 25 October 2017.

Cheka.[194] These officers executed an estimated 100,000 people who they considered enemies of the communist state, effectively winning the civil war for Lenin.[195] Infighting halted in 1922, and Lenin took the first opportunity to unite with fellow European nations Ukraine, Belarus, and Transcaucasia. They signed a treaty on December 30 of that same year, forming the Union of Soviet Socialist Republics, more commonly known as the USSR.

The Russian Empire officially became the Russian Soviet Federative Socialist Republic, and its own capital of Moscow served as the central place of governance for the entire USSR. When Vladimir Lenin died in 1924, his office was obtained by Josef Stalin, a man whose totalitarian regime was responsible for forcing fellow nations to join the union at gunpoint, as well as the mass murder of any citizens who spoke out against him.[196] His strict rule saw heavy investment in Russia's industrial sector which brought the nation wealth and respect throughout Europe and the rest of the world.

Unfortunately for believers in Marx' and Engels' original political doctrine, neither Lenin's nor Stalin's governments and policies mirrored those laid out in the *Communist Manifesto*. Nevertheless, Vladimir Lenin's preserved body lays in public view in Moscow's Red Square. It is a popular attraction for Russians and other international citizens who believe in what he stood for, for the right of all citizens to share in the profits and wealth they help create through labor. Though the ideals of the Russian Revolution were ultimately muted, Lenin's rise to power over the aristocracy gave hope to oppressed workers and reformists all throughout Europe and as far away as the Americas.

---

[194] Leggett, G. *The Cheka: Lenin's political police.* 1981.

[195] "Reasons for the victory of the Reds in the Civil War." *BBC Bitesize.* Web.

[196] Conquest, R. *Stalin: Breaker of Nations.* 1993.

Chapter 25 – World War II

Only the Jew knew that by an able and persistent use of propaganda heaven itself can be presented to the people as if it were hell and, vice versa, the most miserable kind of life can be presented as if it were paradise. The Jew knew this and acted accordingly. But the German, or rather his Government, did not have the slightest suspicion of it. During the War the heaviest of penalties had to be paid for that ignorance.

(Adolf Hitler, *Mein Kampf*)

Fiercely patriotic and disappointed by the outcome of the war, Germans were suffering intensely from widespread starvation. They began rioting on October 29, 1918, and they didn't stop until Kaiser Wilhelm II gave up his crown.[197] He abdicated on November 9, two days before the ceasefire. As for Serbia, it joined Montenegro and other groups of politically displaced Serbs and Croats, eventually forming the Kingdom of Yugoslavia.

In a speech given by Germany's Field Marshal Paul Hindenburg the day after the armistice in November 1918, the German people were told: "You have kept the enemy from crossing our frontiers and you have saved your country from the miseries and disasters of war...We

---

[197] Griffin, Brett. *The Weimar Republic and the Rise of Fascism.* 2017.

end the struggle proudly and with our heads held high where we have stood for four years in the face of a world full of enemies."[198] Despite the patriotic and positive words, the Germans felt they had been betrayed by their politicians. They worked hard to reestablish themselves as a self-governed republic and installed the first President of Germany, Paul Hindenburg, in February of 1919. Since the agreements and negotiations were made in the city of Weimar, the unofficial name for the new political entity was the Weimar Republic. Hindenburg signed the Treaty of Versailles, agreeing to peace alongside those nations who had been his allies and enemies in the war.

The same year Hindenburg took power, a German war veteran named Adolf Hitler joined the German Workers' Party and began sharing his ideas of a purified nation. Hitler believed that Germany should expand its territory by force, curb immigration, and rid itself of Jewish people, and many members of the party agreed with him. In 1920, the group was renamed the National Socialist German Workers' Party, probably in a move to attract more members in a time when socialist ideas appealed to the country's working class.[199] Under Hitler's leadership, the party—whose German initials spelled out NAZI—supported the abandonment of the Treaty of Versailles and rejected the authority of the new Weimer Republic.

Hitler became the leader of the Nazi party by 1921, and two years later, he led the group in the Munich Putsch—a move to overthrow the elected government and establish Germany as a country of race-based citizenship.[200] Hitler's Nazis marched on Berlin but failed to implement their plan. Nine men, including Adolf Hitler, were jailed

---

[198] Martin, Kitchen. "The German Front Experience." *BBC*. Web. 3 October 2011.

[199] "Adolf Hitler." *Holocaust Encyclopedia*. Web.

[200] "Beer Hall Putsch (Munich Putsch.)" *Holocaust Encyclopaedia*. Web.

for their roles in the attempted revolution. Though he was sentenced to five years in prison, Hitler served only eight months. During that time, he wrote the first part of his infamous manifesto, *Mein Kampf* (My Struggle).

Support for Hitler and the Nazis swelled, and in 1932, the party won 37.3 percent of the vote, just behind Hindenburg's nonpartisan administration.[201] Hindenburg awarded Hitler the Chancellorship of the Republic in 1933, giving his former political rival the highest seat of power in the country behind himself.[202] Likely believing this was the best way to appease Nazi voters as well as being able to keep a close eye on Hitler, Hindenburg may have been able to curb the radical behavior of his chancellor except that he died the next year. Hitler abolished the presidency and claimed full political and military power of Germany for himself, under the title of Führer.

The next years of the dictatorship saw Hitler enter into agreements with Italy's Mussolini and Japan's Emperor Hirohito for the purpose of establishing an anti-communist alliance.[203] He even negotiated a naval agreement with Great Britain that allowed for Germany to maintain a large working navy—a right that the Treaty of Versailles had denied. In the latter part of the decade, the Führer began secret plans to begin the expansion of the German Reich (German Realm), starting with Austria. There was a strong Nazi presence in Austria that welcomed Hitler's outreach, but when Hitler tried to pressure Austrian Chancellor Kurt von Schuschnigg into placing those people into the Austrian government, the proposition was declined.[204]

Hitler responded by invading Austria in 1938 and annexing it into the

---

[201] "Adolf Hitler." *Holocaust Encyclopedia.* Web.

[202] Ibid.

[203] "Adolf Hitler Dictator of Germany." *Encyclopaedia Britannica.* Web.

[204] Ibid.

German Reich.[205] Next, he looked toward Czechoslovakia, using his contacts to incite riots by Germans within the foreign realm to make it seem as if his intervention was absolutely necessary. Great Britain's Prime Minister Neville Chamberlain stepped in to offer diplomatic assistance alongside Benito Mussolini, and they supported the annexation of Sudetenland. Sudetenland was a small section of Czechoslovakia in which there were an estimated three million people of German descent, and once the papers were signed, Hitler assured European leaders that he had no desire to expand the Reich further.[206]

It was a complete lie. Later that same year, Hitler swept through the rest of Czechoslovakia, then Prussia and Prague. With his eye on Poland, the Führer considered his options and signed a ten-year nonaggression pact with Joseph Stalin.[207] On September 1, 1939, Hitler invaded Poland, fully understanding that Great Britain and France would oppose him. Both nations declared war on Germany two days later, and Europe was once again at war with itself.

By 1940, Germany had the upper hand in Belgium, the Netherlands, and France, but it had yet to penetrate into Great Britain where Winston Churchill had just been elected prime minister. France surrendered to Nazi occupation, but the continued air attacks on Britain failed to break the Royal Air Force. Thwarted in the west, Hitler turned eastward and attacked the Soviet Union without any heed to his peace agreement. Fortunately for the USSR, Stalin had been preparing for such an event and probably signed the nonaggression agreement to ensure he had time to organize his army. Italy officially joined the war on Germany's side, and Mussolini

---

[205] Ibid.

[206] "Munich Agreement." *Encyclopaedia Britannica.* Web.

[207] "German-Soviet Nonaggression Pact." *Encyclopaedia Britannica.* Web.

began by invading British-held Egypt and British Somaliland.[208]

1941 saw the attack of America's Pearl Harbor by Germany's ally Japan, which spurred the United States into joining the international war.[209] At Stalingrad, the German forces were pushed back with unprecedented strength, but Hitler managed to begin the mass murder of Jewish citizens within Germany and annexed countries. At concentration camps, like the one in Auschwitz, Poland, a diverse mixture of people was imprisoned. These included a majority of Jewish people, as well as homosexuals, gypsies, people with disabilities, communists, trade unionists, Jehovah's Witnesses, anarchists, foreigners, and resistance fighters.[210] These victims and their families were brought in by the thousands to each camp only to be subjected to forced labor. They were starved, beaten, and eventually killed by gunshot or poisonous gas unless dehydration, starvation, overwork, or disease had killed them first.

Italy was successful in annexing Spain, Libya, Croatia, and Montenegro, but the British expelled them from Egypt in a five-day raid.[211] Greece, occupied by Italy since before the outbreak of the war, took the opportunity to push the Axis out of their territory as well. The Allied nations of France, Great Britain, the United States, and the USSR gained little traction against the Nazis until 1944 when they united to invade and liberate Paris and France. The same year, American forces liberated Guam, which had been invaded by Japan.

The Soviets pushed hard from the east and were the first to reach

---

[208] Reynoldson, Fiona and David Taylor. *The Twentieth Century World.* 1998.

[209] Robinson, Bruce. "World War Two: Summary Outline of Key Events." *BBC.* Web. 30 March 2011.

[210] Ridley, Louise. "The Holocaust's Forgotten Victims." *The Huffington Post.* 6 December 2017.

[211] Reynoldson, Fiona and David Taylor. *The Twentieth Century World.* 1998.

Hitler's large concentration camps in Poland by the summer of 1944.[212] They first encountered the Majdanek camp in July and were horrified to discover the gas chambers left behind by hastily retreating Nazi soldiers. The Axis had tried to cover the evidence of mass murder by burning the camp, but they were unsuccessful. Soviet forces discovered similar setups at a succession of abandoned camps, including Belzec and Treblinka. In January of 1945, they found Auschwitz and freed the 7,500 prisoners who remained there. In April, American forces freed 20,000 Jewish hostages from the Buchenwald camp in Germany; the British liberated Bergen-Belson soon afterward and found 60,000 prisoners there.[213] Ten thousand of those died within a week of liberation due to typhus, starvation, and other illnesses.[214] In total, 17 million people were killed in the concentration camps, and 6 million of them were of the Jewish faith.[215]

Benito Mussolini was captured and killed on April 28, 1945, by an Italian resistance force determined to free its country from fascism and Nazi coercion.[216] The Soviets swept into Berlin that same week, and when Hitler realized his ally was dead and there was no escape, he killed himself with both a cyanide pill and a gunshot to the head on April 30.[217] His partner, Eva Braun, died alongside him, having eaten a cyanide pill.[218] On May 7, Germany officially surrendered.

Japan, however, was still in action and actively invading China while

---

[212] "Liberation of Nazi Camps." *Holocaust Encyclopedia.* Web.

[213] Ibid.

[214] Ibid.

[215] Enyia, Samuel O. *Servant Leadership.* 2018.

[216] Haugen, Brenda. *Benito Mussolini: Fascist Italian Dictator.* 2007.

[217] Layton, Donald. *World War II: A Global Perspective.* 1998.

[218] Ibid.

the Allies invaded the Japanese island of Iwo Jima. The Allies discussed invading the Japanese mainland but were concerned about casualties. The new American President, Harry Truman, offered a different plan: a nuclear bomb. On August 6, one such bomb was dropped on Hiroshima; on the 9, a second was dropped on Nagasaki. The first explosion killed at least 90,000 people, while the second killed at least 39,000.[219]

Japan surrendered on August 15, 1945, and World War II was finished. An estimated 50 to more than 80 million people were killed in the fighting.[220]

---

[219] Rhoads, Sean and Brooke McCorkle. *Japan's Green Monsters*. 2018.

[220] Robinson, Bruce. "World War Two: Summary Outline of Key Events." *BBC*. Web. 30 March 2011.

Chapter 26 - The Cold War Era

James Burnham's theory has been much discussed, but few people have yet considered its ideological implications—that is, the kind of world-view, the kind of beliefs, and the social structure that would probably prevail in a state which was at once unconquerable and in a permanent state of "cold war" with its neighbors.

(George Orwell)[221,222]

In the aftermath of the Second World War, Germany was divided into two nations: the capitalist West and the communist East. Berlin was split right down the middle, and traveling between the two fiercely nationalistic sides was very dangerous. Much of Eastern Europe remained under the growing influence of the Soviet Union, East Germany included, while the western nations looked toward the United States as an emerging superpower. Though they had been allies in both wars, the US and the USSR developed a deep distrust of one another that turned into a multi-decade feud known as the Cold War. Both nations funded nuclear testing and began storing the kind of weapons that had devastated Japan in 1945.

Many Eastern European nations that had received help from Soviet forces during both wars were easily convinced to convert to Russia's

---

[221] "You and the Atomic Bomb." *Tribune.* 19 October 1945.

[222] George Orwell's article, first appearing in London's *Tribune,* was the first to use the term "cold war."

style of communism and join the USSR. Within the first few years of peace, East Germany was joined in its alliance with the Soviet Union by Bulgaria, Czechoslovakia, Hungary, Poland, and Romania. These, combined with Ukraine, Estonia, Armenia, Azerbaijan, Belarus, Georgia, Moldova, Latvia, and nearby Asian countries, formed the so-called Iron Curtain.[223]

The Iron Curtain, a term used to refer to the wall of European socialist countries between Russia and Western Europe, was first used by British Prime Minister Winston Churchill in 1946.[224] The term didn't only refer to the political separation between capitalist, democratic nations and communist nations, but it also referred to the idealism that they represented. On the eastern side of the curtain, citizens were subjected to communist propaganda via the radio waves; on the western side, they were fed anti-communist propaganda. *Radio Free Europe* attempted to provide its eastern listeners with western news broadcasts, but they were continuously interrupted by radio jammers in the east.[225]

The political reorganization of Europe and its colonial holdings in the Middle East and Africa inspired the people of Ireland to demand their own independence from Great Britain. In 1948, the Republic of Ireland Act removed the bulk of the Irish island from Commonwealth control.[226] By Easter Monday of the next year, the deed was complete. A small northeastern corner remained within the Great British kingdom, known as Northern Ireland. Within that small piece of mainland Ireland, a majority of Protestants and pro-UK unionists

---

[223] Pipes, Richard E. et al. "Soviet Union, Historic State, Eurasia." *Encyclopaedia Britannica*. Web.

[224] Ibid.

[225] Ibid.

[226] "Surprise move from Free State status to independent republic." *Irish Times*. 5 April 1999.

preferred to stay linked to the Church of England and the unified state.

Northern Ireland was still home to nationalists, however, and these became active in the Irish Republican Army (IRA). The IRA was responsible for hundreds of terrorist attacks within Northern Ireland and England in the hopes that it would convince both entities to remove Northern Ireland from the Commonwealth. As Great Britain and Ireland waged their own small-scale warfare, so too did the Western world against the Soviet Union. There were no formal battles between the USSR and Western Europe or, the USSR's main perceived enemy, the United States of America, but the two ideologically divided sides managed to draw battle lines in an astonishing number of proxy wars between 1945 and 1990.

The first of these wars took place in China and Greece, with each country suffering a civil war between communist groups and non-socialist republicans. In the first case, the communist forces—supported by the Soviet Union in terms of political organization, military expertise, and weapons—were victorious in setting up the People's Republic of China.[227] The United States, having offered similar support to the Republic of China, failed in its efforts there. In Greece, however, the US and anti-communist Greek parties won the war, culminating in a loss for Soviet-backed parties. The two countries pitted themselves strategically against one another in this manner more than 70 times during the Cold War. The majority of the fighting took place outside North America and Europe, in countries such as Korea, Vietnam, and the Philippines.

The struggle for ideological supremacy didn't only manifest itself on the battlegrounds of foreign nations. It also changed the way the Soviet Union and the United States prioritized national projects, like the development of space-age technology. The Space Race was the name given to the unofficial competition between American and

---

[227] Chang, H.H. Chang. *Chiang Kai Shek – Asia's Man of Destiny*. 2007.

Soviet governments to fund the most advanced and successful outer space exploration team. The results were quite exciting, despite the underlying tension found in citizens, media outlets, and military engagements.

Much of the technology used at the start of the Space Race had been developed for use in rockets during WWII, and both sides had a great deal of information to build a foundation for the burgeoning science. Espionage between Soviets and Americans also had a hand in the exchange of this information, in part thanks to the British spies of the secretly Soviet-aligned Cambridge Five. On October 4, 1957, the Soviets launched the first satellite—Sputnik—into space. [228] The next year, following a failed satellite launch in 1957, the United States placed Explorer 1 in orbit.[229] It had a rudimentary communications system attached to it where data could be gathered and retrieved. That same year, the National Aeronautics and Space Administration organization was founded, better known as NASA. Via NASA, the United States ran ahead of its rival and began planning a manned mission to outer space while simultaneously launching a spy satellite. The Soviet Union pushed back and launched the first man into space, Yuri Gagarin, on April 12, 1961. Back in the German capital, the Berlin Wall was constructed, further solidifying the demarcation between West and East.[230] United States President John Fitzgerald Kennedy visited West Berlin in 1963 and made an impassioned speech to crowds there, declaring Berlin (ostensibly West Berlin in particular) to be a city of all free men.

Two thousand years ago, the proudest boast was civis romanus sum ["I am a Roman citizen."] Today, in the world of freedom,

---

[228] Crompton, Samuel Willard. *Sputnik/Explorer I: The Race to Conquer Space.* 2007.

[229] Ibid.

[230] Schwartz, Harold. *Outpost Berlin.* 2010.

the proudest boast is *"Ich bin ein Berliner!"*[231]

By 1966, the Soviets had built a craft that orbited the moon and landed there. The ultimate goal—landing humans safely on the moon—was first achieved by NASA in 1969 when the Apollo 11 mission touched down and returned home with all three astronauts intact. Throughout the 1970s and 1980s, more countries joined in on the efforts to develop space technology and make their own marks on the industry. Canada, France, Great Britain, China, and Japan were the first to do so, and in 1975, the European Space Agency was formed.[232]

Cold War tensions cooled somewhat during the 1970s and were reignited in the 1980s until the administration of a new Soviet leader changed everything: Mikhail Gorbachev. Gorbachev made concerted efforts to restructure the Soviet Union into a fairer system of government, and he gracefully let go of European member states whose own political systems were under intense pressure to change. The Iron Curtain metaphorically fell, and under extreme pressure from defecting East Germans who refused to cross back into East Germany, Gorbachev allowed the network of communism around his country to fall apart. On the 9th of November, 1989, new regulations were announced in Berlin that allowed for travel through the wall, to and from both sides.[233]

The announcement was on the news multiple times that very night in both East and West Germany. People on both sides began to climb the Brandenburg Gate within hours of learning the new regulations.[234] Overwhelming guards on both sides, the waves of unified Germans

---

[231] John F. Kennedy quoted by Gavin Esler. *Lessons from the Top.* 2012.

[232] Cogen, Marc. *An Introduction to European Intergovernmental Organizations.* 2015.

[233] Sebetsyen, Victor. *Revolution 1989: The Fall of the Soviet Empire.* 2009.

[234] Manghani, Sunil. *Image Critique and the Fall of the Berlin Wall.* 2008.

flooded over the wall and began chipping it apart. Soon, bulldozers came to destroy the dividing line and start the journey back to unification. At midnight on October 3, 1990, East Germany was formally dissolved, and its citizens were welcomed back into the unified Federal Republic of Germany.[235] After the dissolution of the Soviet Union a little over a year later in 1991, the Cold War was finally over.

---

[235] Sauvain, Philip. *Key Themes of the 20th Century.* 1996.

Epilogue

As Europe entered the second half of the 20th century, many of its nations decided to work toward a stronger unity throughout the continent. In the years immediately following the end of WWII, Europe's political minds worked together to start the coalition that would become the European Union. Six countries founded the group: Belgium, the Netherlands, Luxembourg, France, West Germany, and Italy. With Germany reunification, the push for EU membership became a priority for much of Europe, including former Soviet countries. As of 2019, the European Union has 28 member states, though the United Kingdom is currently undergoing an exit negotiation.[236]

Warfare has by no means ceased in Europe after the horrors of both World Wars or the multitude of civil wars that followed, though it has not nearly matched the devastation of those conflicts. Modern Europe is a land of rich cultural history and technological advancement that exists side by side. The diverse communities of the continent have never forgotten the stories of their ancestors, nor have they ignored the lessons of their violent past. As Europe continues to move forward in the 21st century, it remains a beacon of knowledge and humility to the rest of the world.

---

[236] The 28 member countries of the EU." *European Union.* Web.

Check out another book by Captivating History

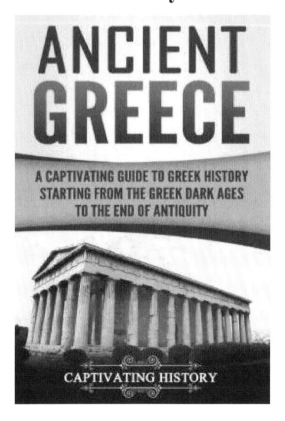

Free Bonus from Captivating History
(Available for a Limited time)

Hi History Lovers!

Now you have a chance to join our exclusive history list so you can get your first history ebook for free as well as discounts and a potential to get more history books for free! Simply visit the link below to join.

Captivatinghistory.com/ebook

Also, make sure to follow us on Facebook, Twitter and Youtube by searching for Captivating History.

Printed in Great Britain
by Amazon

58500038R00085